MW01426898

For Peter
Best Wishes

Book of Leaves

Conwenna Stokes

COACH HOUSE BOOKS   TORONTO

Copyright © 1998 by Jay MillAr

CANADIAN CATALOGUING IN PUBLICATION DATA

Millar, Jay, 1971-
   The Ghosts of Jay MillAr

Contents: Book of leaves : from The ghosts of Jay MillAr / Conwenna Stokes – Bur'd : from The ghosts of Jay MillAr / Alex Cayce – Heartrants : from The ghosts of Jay MillAr / H. Azel – Perfectly ordinary dreams : from The ghosts of Jay MillAr / James Llar – Short g(hosts : from The ghosts of Jay MillAr / John Elliott.

ISBN 1-55245-034-1

I. Title.

PS8576.I3157G46 1998   C811'.54   C98-931301-8
PR9199.3.M.45693G46 1998

If you don't like poetry don't write poetry.

if you don't like poets don't be a poet,
but feel free to write as much poetry as you like.

there is a difference.

any community is fictional
as is what might be
gathered randomly within the landscape
and the witchcraft available at all times
could even cause the greatest of trees
to burst into leaves one day.

it's that easy

if you don't believe in witchcraft you
couldn't possibly hope to exist.

can't deal 'em ya can't play,
everything falls but the game goes on.

    J.M.

☆ Tree Culture – Some Field Notes [1]

APPENDAGES: Not the branches, which are part of the body of the tree. Unlike many other species, tree appendages are not directly connected to the body, like the fingers, the breasts, or the penis of mammals. Careful observation revealed that each tree community has its prey and predators, its decomposers and recyclers, its planters and harvesters, its mechanics, its writers, nests, artists, leaves and musicians. These are the appendages of the tree. While they may spend some time physically attached to the tree, for the most part they are in fact entirely separate beings, free to migrate away from the tree itself, like satellites with a chosen place of residence. It is through these living satellites that communication between trees is possible.

ART: Mild gentle brush strokes. Glory.

CHILDHOOD: As with every species, the childhood of trees is pure witchcraft.[2] Worship of the sun. Worship of the rain. Worship of the earth, the wind, the clouds. Worship of the grubs, the birds, the squirrels, the chipmunks, the rattlesnakes, the rabbits, the deer, the butterflies, the nuts, the *praying mantis*, the woodpeckers. Worship of the world and meditation on fire.

DREAMS: Contrary to popular belief, the dreams of trees are not located beneath the surface of the earth mingled among the roots as a kind of 'ghost tree'. The roots of any species of tree are simply roots, as the earth in which they live is simply earth. This idea of 'hidden dreams' has been a misconception of popular culture for some time now, not only in regard to trees, but with most creatures of the planet. And while having some clever features, such as the metaphor of the 'underground' (ref. Greek mythology) or the subconscious, it is only a limited vision. Once again humans have managed to overlook the obvious. Trees are themselves dreams.[3] We believe this because they obviously communicate in images, as opposed to speech. What they dream is of their own mind and anyone or thing that comes in contact with them. As the leaves of the deciduous are shed during the final months of the year the various dream states of the tree fall away one by one, until the very centre of the dream is exposed. Conifers, on the other hand, live entirely masked in a dream, and can never be awakened. It is difficult to view the exact centre of any deciduous tree's dream state, even in winter, when all the leaves have fallen. This is due to the natural masking qualities of snow. Just before the leaves return it is possible to catch a glimpse.

FALLING: It is as though the tree had become wise enough to teach its children a thing or two about mortality.[4] We believe that this is why trees are capable of outliving almost every species on the Earth[5], the only close exception being the great sea turtle.

MIGRATION: (Time Travel via the emotions) Since it is consciousness that gives root to The Tree, migration occurs whenever there is no trace of consciousness present within a three kilometer radius. In the case of such an absence, trees are free to voyage throughout the world by phasing in and out of time upon any available frequencies. This was discovered only recently after careful observation of specific trees grown in a semi-vacuous state. These trees, unable to recognize any forms of consciousness nearby, allowed observers to witness their ghost-like appearance, the mysterious translucence of leaves shifting in time. Most trees, however, actually fear migration and time travel of any kind, and are much more comfortable in a permanent 'rooted' state. This is the reason why they invite many creatures to actively live their lives in and about them. One should not ignore the species of renegade trees, however, those who choose to live in harsh conditions (cold regions, high altitudes, and the like). These are the solitary dream-travellers, who wish for solitude, shifting through the space of time and wind.

PHILOSOPHY: They are your thoughts. Think them. No One Cares. Safety in numbers. Think.

POETRY: As far as can be determined, the poetry of trees contains no known words recognizable in any language of the human race.[6] It has been determined to be quite punctual in nature, and often it is up to any creatures who live within their branches to become their voice. This reveals the humble nature of trees, as anyone who hears this poetry will tend to assume it is the authors who are reciting it. Trees are in a sense ghost writers of the permanent kind, and wish to remain anonymous, using whatever pseudonyms available in the surrounding environment. Although it is mostly speculation, the poetry of trees is both open, in a kind of gentle explosive manner, and self-reflective, in a violent implosive manner. This is to say that the poetry of trees moves inwardly and outwardly at the exact same moment, which may also help to explain why trees appear not to move.

SEX / SEXUAL PRACTICES: *Each tree is a long slow orgasm of summer.* Deciduous trees are generally more sexually satisfied at the end of the summer months and are therefore too tired to maintain their foliage during the winter months. As long as they have leaves, however, these trees are entirely female. Only after their leaves are shed do they become male. Conifers are therefor female for the entire year, and are constantly in a state of orgasm. Thus the social interaction between trees in most forests is lesbian in nature. One will notice easily, walking casually through a woodlot during the summer, the soft leafy curves and gentle swaying motion of trees bathed in their leaves, as though they were walking sensuously through a dream. One will not notice this during the winter. Because conifers remain female throughout the long winter, this allows for a certain amount of heterosexual interaction throughout those months. It has been recorded that the temperature in the middle of a mixed forest will always remain a few degrees higher than a forest entirely made up of deciduous, or coniferous trees. However, this does not mean that trees prefer heterosexual activity to lesbianism; it is more that they enjoy a certain amount of variety within the forest. One can also experience the noticeable difference between the atmospheres caused by standing naked in a forest during the middle of summer and rolling naked in the snow of a forest at the height of winter.

SCIENCE: There are no tree scientists. Yet we understand that they are extremely wise and spend most of their lives pondering the nature of their being. When they reach a certain age, they also begin to contemplate the nature of their being as it pertains to those creatures around them. There is a heightened awareness about a mature forest that cannot be denied.

SKIN: Trees are undoubtedly all skin, down to the heart, naked as air. It becomes most noticeable as the leaves, which are not skin at all, but a kind of mental clothing7, are shed from the deciduous. This leaves the outer, fragmented layers of their rough skin and genitals exposed for several months. Some species of the coniferous, however, have admitted that their needles are not only a mental sheath, but are an outer sheath of the skin. This allows other creatures of the local environment, even other trees, to live partially, or entirely, within their being for the entire year. We can only assume this enveloping nature is the same for the deciduous, but are fairly positive that this is the case at least for the months of spring and summer. It is strange, however, that despite their apparent shyness, it was the conifers who were willing to offer information about their culture, while the more exhibitionist deciduous declined any such information.

TREE SONGS: Tree songs are always songs of prayer. Variations on the word 'wish' usually make up most of the songs and have been heard both in person and from recordings made on hidden tape recorders (examples: 'whoosh', 'shush', or 'wiiiith'). To whom or what these songs are directed has yet to be determined.[8] Yet we feel that those who receive such songs are grateful, for it cannot be denied that trees live the most benevolent of lives.[9]

TELEPATHY: (   )

WORK: The work of trees is socio–political in nature, for obvious reasons.[10] Not only do trees live in the community of the forest, but there is also a community of leaves gathered upon each tree. Trees discovered very early that they could live most peacefully in a fourth dimensional system, which is why they evolved as they have. Leaves are all equal and are free to live as they please, while the wooden structure of their trees differ only in size, age, shape, and species, perfectly capable of living their lives as they wish. Each tree of the forest is also free to live as they please, in as much as they maintain their leaves to the best of their ability. The leaves of each tree are in fact eternal to the extent that the tree upon which they exist continues to live. Even though the leaves of deciduous trees fall away throughout the months of autumn, in no way does any leaf die until the entire tree dies, and each one is reincarnated as a leaf in exactly the same place of each branch. This system is essentially the same for conifers, although their leaves, or needles, fall away and are reincarnated throughout the year. It is in this way that the tree can care for each of its leaves equally and fairly, while the leaves may work together for the benefit of the tree, and for any of the tree's many appendages. It has taken trees millions of years to develop this political system, and maintaining it for the benefit of all levels of life is what the tree considers its labor. We are confident that they are doing a fine job of it, simply because individuals cannot help feeling wonderfully easy going and free when in the presence of such beings.

☆   *Trees*

The undeniable, satisfactory crunch
        of the sky through the leaves
              that falls to catch our place,

how I would love to be able to roll
        the words off my tongue
            like branches that go on

forever. The trees say
      our leaves are small and we move our feet
            in time to the winds that sing

too softly for you to hear.
      A Dream in absolute knowledge,
          the very heart of the tree where

no birds sing. They say each bird
        was made to sing its own song,
            different from the others,

and yet the same. They say each branch
        was meant to hold a different bird
            each singing a different song.

Out here my head is as low
       to the ground as a root.
           Our breath disappears

with each passing moment,
      a high pitched wail we do not hear
            restoring us to consciousness.

☆ TreeSong

In this empty landscape we have gathered successfully (one house) among the leaves that float for miles along the sky and the leaves that go with them. What riches we have are of home. An acoustic guitar in the mouth of the sun. And passing... I was an oak and you were a birch. This clear dark sky has been preserved here for all time in a version of itself (VIEW). And we live in the sun, we live in the wind. Painting our symbols for the eyes of our lovers. I was a maple and you were a poplar. We live in the rain. Married to the very thought of the wind to life. Satie would have been proud. Just look at the stars. I was a sycamore and you were a red ash. We were so ashamed to fuck like writhing snakes in our upper branches during the long hot summers that as we waited for winter we would fall apart. We would sleep so hard, like rocks or ice, just to cover up the scent of our bondage. What leaves we have shed in the months of our offering. To each other and ourselves. I was a hawthorn and you were a willow. One or two of our beasts will float forever upon their thrones like downy pebbles; we let them have their stay, in the end we give them such defeat. We only know these gifts. Beethoven would have been proud. Of course we were living together, and all in love. All summer I enjoyed listening to the clacking of your leaves and I have fought against each day from that perspective. I was a downy serviceberry and you were a sumac. In autumn, why do we always fall for ourselves? There is something entirely justified and hopeless about our situation. Love would have been proud. Living like cradles poking into the sky, always giving up gently at the last possible second. I was a hickory and you were an evergreen. We have all been offered such riches. But that is what I love about you. So much like myself. So hopeless, full of curiosity about this language we stick into each other as we die of love and hope. Living in the fallout of winter. I was a magnolia and you were a slippery elm. Sometimes there could be miles and miles of us, all holding hands, pierced through the many hearts of the rain. Holding each creature inside us like this soft wood pulp. Satie would have been proud. All of us alone together and unnoticed. Our own path is no less than where we let ourselves fall. Often it is how we wonder why we do this. I was a white cedar and you were a dogwood. No reason, no worry, listen to the last songbirds of summer sing our way.

✿ LeafSong

      Because the two sides of our love, invisible, opaque
      we will always love We will never   We love you... O
                      what love
    We always love. Use us accordingly O seasonal beasts, for
    we shall be our ghosts until we return filled with green.
      We remember with winter   space we never leave.

      Make love to air and fall away   what we are
            Small beings in love with you
      O ground, love you and shall wait for you
   always over here, on our side, alive living with you O air,
we are   will be the wind one more time   waiting in the wind
in the wind   the birth of the wind...   many shapes of wind and home.
Through the burning hot days of summer which is the fruit of our lust.
    Waiting where we are   we are for what   we come with us
    where we know we are.   Here we are wet, here we are green

      awaiting your solid kisses   O ground, slide through us
        as we melt into   All summer long in the air,
   the hot wind our shape flows through us with motion our soft
        limitations. Lead grace to the slow orgasm of the tree
        when we turn to the light birds ourselves.
      What advice might we give   We become
             our red shapes
for such   to kiss. kiss our yellow shapes. kiss our brown gold shapes.
   As we become   ghosts never disappear. We long to with you,
    O ground, for you fall through us.   For we know who

      we will always be   here in love with you O air,
        even in the lust our absence,
    When we make love to ground. O ground,
    all summer long, we are in love with you,
         waiting for   return.

✩ 4 Leaves (4 pages)

when the wind is all around so
stoned i couldn't possibly move. (BUT I DO)
What intellect could be out here in the open
bug-eyed, sapped out of my mind.

might as well be on a bicycle. turn over and
over myself, move along without trying.
out here the ups and downs are accompanied
by hills that meet the dark edges of the air

where we will slice at what creates hanging
on, and i bite my nails to rid them of a dance
they will always choose, the ritual of their time.
I have also thought it must be easy to ride without hands.

Ah! everything tends to become directional with time, and drawn
off the deep end.   (settle down and be where).
i know it really has nothing to do with me, but
with a small thing of myself that i live.

what could i be without you? i'm pretty worn out
of sight against the wind and amongst our many shapes,
as they come into being and not at all yet drifting on
the slope of darkness you should call night.

which of course, as anyone with
half a heart will tell you,
will only go down from here on
in through slippery shadows of air.

it's all folk music
of the　　　　air,
or something similar,

a quiet imitation,
a quiet right through the trees
of the trees

beating the thickness
of wood, something
that goes on

a bright heavy
summer, a gun full
of heat that rolls

the wind, so slow,
going nowhere into the night.
i find it so, i don't know,

perfect, this balance
between heaven and sky.
the unceremonial heaven of leaves,

being down, pulls thusly, thusly
and is soft, near the roots,
i imagine the few of us, caught

pressed flowers, holding on branches,
we are so full of sorrow and beauty
that much could be regret.

we are filled with the cold
air of two lovers
and Glory.

birds dart from second to second
and we flutter, wait for what moment

(breathe)

what thoughts have we, what lives
yes, we have thought *fuck you*

in forest ways, and creatures
drunk on their own ways, go on

and hide with us, gather us up, as we
grow old and vision fades until we are blind

until we are those creatures
as we turn with the earth, and how

(breath)

with wind and rain and sun and birds
each a piece of weather, what thoughts

our lives

it's fine to fall, fine to drift as thought
it were memory you feed upon (wits)

dumb radical cool breeze (behavior)
falls through what if the greengrey air were black

that is the city, where we wake, and
storing up for winter, nuts, (undertow) bolts,

sounds of busses and of cars, all the drift as though
and the movement beyond, light birds (dead soldiers

come to life) presumably the small ones, periodically
outside, light panic rules air going on leave

then one long string of (notes)

are anyone who
falls against their own breath
feels us here
listens carefully
who knows will disappear

are anyone who is going
are speaking like they do

anyone who is soft
against their own skin
like nests

are watching
care about
only know such gifts

what dark we have caught in branches (sleeves)
all day, dark, and more here. dark

piled up light as all those who sleep
while we do not. forever asleep, dark
ourselves (the text is black on us

(we never write) and we never forget)
any dream of the day in our lives. we

                (RIpPle)

are what dark is in the light of (this
ink) the trunk's white skin. forever
asleep, we are awake and piled high

sink into the dream's great earth

.... 11

these flakes fall
cover

☆ Leaf Legend

FOR EACH LEAF

a star

they are so

here

☆ *The Present Today is Built from the Past*[12]

                                                                           Equinox '96

stupid it is to run from the weather, the sun, the clouds, as
falling leaves the air dry, all the brittle stars against those
seasons that pass daily[13] as though they were out to get you: remember
it takes two to linger in conversation, the rest is just thought
and it's all the same thing. we take warmer blankets now, and dream
more often, alive, meeting strange out of the way breathing, slower now,
noticing the dream was just awake staring at the window[14], a decrease
in pressure, the heat easing off, so obvious to everyone, everything
present to remind us that the world is not here with you in it.
think about it and we will linger on edge, imagine, noting what
there is, as abstractions we are left to ourselves, to preach, to meditate
on what to consume and exhume, rolling along that slant again,
of faces brown against the sky after the sun, tired, we who survived.
light.   trees.   a window.   7:45 a.m.
and we are nowhere at all[15] : summer has come to an end again.
stand back. slow down. all of this is what we have longed for
as memory speeds up into the top of our skull to slice at the crisp
they find there, and it's all the same thing. we have been here
before doing this very thing, as though the very multitude of flannel
were a slow leak reservoir heaven of warmth to bathe every inch of
your mind. the heat is suddenly mindfuck't again: and it's over.
and it's over as autumn shoots each leaf through their memory so
ancient they all turn to colour and dust[16]… we miss things constantly;
think behind each thing, look around still blocked from the sunlit
voice of abstraction itself, left with what we began with in our minds
to begin with and discover nostalgia here in the present   i was
once a small creature in my sunday best and the light fell just so, as
did my feet, walking, there in the present,[17] the squirrels, the sun,
the leaves and the small birds sputtering across rooftops, the books
under my arm. i have been here before. a caravan, riding at dawn,
looking through the wood and preparing for winter, the bear, the rabbit,
the deer, the chipmunk, remembering paths we took, our subtle repetitions,

the smooth essence of memory[18] and looking through the stupid window can make us believe there really is a world out there, as opposed to in here, where all our different minds, all our past incarnations fuse into sunlight.

☆ *Sneezing Out There Rips My Head*[19]

                wide open.

the rush of the trees in the wind, being the essence of trees
is what allows myself the end of the wind that will never arrive

in the present. i just don't want to meet it out there tonight.
one can listen to the sound and know the secret lives of trees, their passage

in this, a time of small gods who sing with the wind and of it.
constantly i feel this mounting and then the lethargy…   all the time…

O how I could spit like the wind tonight, venom, all the stupid rush of reason,
godly sounds, the wishes, the grunts, the mischief, Love… i have found love
squelches at these days repeating their habits endlessly. yet it is the
lethargy i have trouble with in the midst of such kafuffle. makes
me wish it were Sunday afternoon instead of Wednesday night, when spirits
aren't all grown up with nowhere to hide from the many disappointments
where we are. i look forward to being contained by the mounting of love,

as it continues listening to the trees as they never end despite
my own sad reflections of living. trees in the darkness reach

out what branches. branches i have never seen until
we are ready to embark into the wind.

                we are ready to embark into

always it's against where we are in the present and now the breeze
against my arms pincushion and cool. so lovely i could almost cry to

                    imagine...

all those days of summer might return, driving through the small towns of
South Western Ontario: Watford, Thamesville, Chatham, Tilbury, Belle River;
i always love to see the skies there through the tiny intersections as they
fall gently to touch the earth. there were many photo opportunities.

driving through the intersection of each town, passing earthclad tattered beings
blowing in the wind. how i love them so... how they are made up as if from the
elements themselves, breathing what air. i could almost become one of them
i love to see them crossing the street. their own way of space and speech. every
stupid thing i've ever done nags against this landscape. which is, of course, my
Mind. my unlikeliness of ever succeeding. the big brash and hopeless city
where i live. i might be impressed (in fact i am) by how my own memories begin
in a rural landscape. years ago, working farms near Lucan Ontario shoveling
horseshit from the stalls of rich horses with my brother Darren, the stench of
piss and flies, loading up the wagons of hay with Darren and Steve, piling row
after row of sweetgreen hay, each wagon piled so high, each of our own energy,
the roll of the land, the bump of the wagon, the sky touching...

                    it is so nice to look there

and find yourself, and know you were once full of who you were, or could be,
and in such looking you are still youthful. who you are. all day long
in the stupid heat, until the day was cool to the touch
and the hay was in our lungs, heavy with sweat and diesel fuel under the rich
evening skies I would care to remember in later years and write about in
poems. big dumb poems that would try to capture in the language
a kind of wind that opens up the sky.[20]

            (Our minds glass eyes and mist, youthful, on fire with being...)

poetry would eventually become a means to branch into the past by plundering
the present, the future moment shifting in and out of the wind, leaves less violent
than a sneeze and just as satisfying. it's the same thing that left me
wondering for days just how many times i could write about leaves without

                boring the reader to death.

i will naturally want to equate this with those Sunday afternoons about the house.
they were all of light. even in the dark cool house they were
bright and clear. never did i want to sleep so much. you can still see what
they're like by looking at the sky when the light white clouds hold the sunlight
in a cup. all of clear breezes. nothing to do. nothing, the making of poetry.
we were going about our business, what sweet schoolkid lives, clear and twisting,
O, so, lazy. secrets were hidden away in lost photo albums. once the fire
burns away these lives, what memories could be lost forever?

        it was our duty to watch the windows do whatever.

we were thinking... what thoughts... asleep or otherwise.
windows were a lot like television back then, only somewhat slower. there
was less information but it appeared on a wider scale, more dots per square inch,
melt, vibrate, sit or shatter, open them up to the cool wind, feel. these
were things we learned in the cool house where people live. we live there, days
days and days. still do. in our head. walk right up and fall asleep. it
was before i walked out to the back lot to watch the flakes of snow
miss the branches to fall upon my belly. i was still pushing the mower
across each square inch of the landscape near the house. here, the
incense continually seeks only to remind me of autumn.
imagine between the summer and the winter what changes.   what changes.
leaves and lawns and wind, is this what i...

        in the afternoon

after school we would fall asleep in order to record my dreams
in a small yellow notebook. we were walking the lanes of a highway. we were
all one being, i remember, and inside each of us we were happy, on the road,
each of us in our own lane. peaceful curves along the soft rubber–like pavement.
each footstep was the pure bliss of a hopeless grin. a motion. a leaf
or mote of dust caught in the sunny cross–fire of a breeze. we were
moving at the speed of rabbits or of elk, and were perfectly
capable of switching to other lanes, but only if we wished for such a

thing to happen. we were all completely in control, there was no reason to
disturb this world as it had been presented to us. gentle as it was.

      there were many beautiful photo opportunities.

and i couldn't wake up, aware that i was shaking slightly, that i was
asleep and dreaming, totally awake, aware that i was. i was everything
of that dream, everything of that room, everything of that landscape
i was to find myself in at this moment.   it was a fine cocoon of…
i admit i was a little terrified, for i had never experienced paralysis like that. looking at
myself now from the doorway in the sun, from the outside or the future,
i see this memory curled up in a brown–golden leaf, a figure lying
on the bed like that, what youth, so feeble, so full of noise. this is the past
andthe future meeting in the dull landscape of Ontario: Memories
so quick they do not happen. and yet these are what we, here, as the sun gives
way to the cold nights, rely upon for warmth. i look at myself from the doorway
in the sun and we are always dreaming about the various highways of my
life, where i was, where it was we were taking ourselves, where we were

      between places and the sound

of the wind and the radio. sitting in the back seat of the car with my
brothers. as it was, we were destined to find ourselves day after day
travelling back and forth across the landscape of that country during the
summer. we were human thought crunching along the road, ready to stop at
any time to look. moving at the speed of trees, our faces in the wind of the
open window, reaching out with the stillness of the mind. that wind,
it lifts up my heart that way by the gentle removal of one or two ribs.
all these gaping holes where we have been. awake and dreaming, alive
and dead, everything and nothing, home and away. the rock slides stand

      so still, what creates a pattern in the human mind.

the back roads of South Western Ontario so deep within my back,
rolling up and down my spine, the tiny mice, mushroom the size of
my head. how many times have i been in the woods near Tilbury Ontario, noticing

how the leaves have changed ever so slightly over the period of a month.
how many times have i driven past the ostrich farm there, and past
the small, flat graveyards and the slanting gas stations?
Sunday afternoon mosquito buzz jazz monotone. Windsor Ontario
would eventually become a heightening of my own consciousness, a long drive
that allows old friends to find each other at the end of the country. The Bruce
Peninsula under my knees. resin and rainwater, chipmunks and rattlesnakes.
every species imaginable will eat out of your palm there, take what you
give them. (thank you). the cliff we climbed up from Miller Lake grew smaller
every time we returned, became less of an adventure, more of dreamfact, the birch
trees would shrink over the years yet we could still peel the bark away
in large, paper–like strips to start the fire. in a rowboat with my dad
and the mist as the sun appears. it was about five a.m. I'm sure this
is a place in Eastern Canada, though in my mind it has various qualities
like that of a dream. wide awake. just as the sun opens up the fog a crack.
dad rows the boat and my hand drags through the blackish salt water
to the sounds of such strings. Point Peelee is here too, undoubtedly
beneath the soles of my feet. Matt and i spent hours skipping stones into
the flat grey surface of Lake Erie while Hazel gathered shells and rocks
polished by time into her skirt. in the water where we meet ourselves by
chance along the way, speaking to the various species of birds present
there at seven in the morning watching no, feeling the wind rustling through
the lush foliage. Western Canada somewhere not entirely transparent,
ever, never ever there. each morning i would rise at five a.m. to check
the trap lines, sometimes sitting and watching the pinkish clouds hover
above the cool wet morning conifers and rockslides like old gods reborn and
walking between the mountains. during the day i would race the ridiculous
silver RVs up and down the hills on a borrowed bike, i could finally feel
small in the midst of the world, so huge i could choke on the wind.
hiking up the sides of mountains i would stop for a moment to look down through
the lake to see the very centre of its cool gravity, you could sit there and
concentrate openly listening to the ominous call of the pika
hiding among the rocks, the very creature my father had studied for years in that
landscape. yes, i say, raising my hand, i am present and looking around.

and where am i?

i find in the end but what am i to make of all my feelings? i might think of
my first memory but it is ALL memory. all those highschool weekends on
mushrooms with Matt, on mushrooms with Peter. on mushrooms with Chuck,
walking the streets of London Ontario, at the cottage watching the lake just
sitting there, shining in the forever setting summer sun and angling the air,
we were all looking down the road, it seems, all the time,
squinting to see ahead. as far as we could see. i would find myself
years later down that road in a room with Hazel, Stefan, Rob,
Joe, and Sue, all of us on mushrooms. even now, looking down these roads
there is nothing there…   nothing…   looking at myself
now from the doorway in the sun. it all becomes comforting.
it all becomes the same thing while i am busy waiting out the while of each moment.
what happens but what has happened? which branch should we sit on, looking
at how far it recedes into the future? we were amazed

at how far we had come, at how we had arrived, and still are. amazed.
looking at the sun, or at the leaves falling peacefully in front of the Runnymede
United Church, November 12, 1996, 11:42 pm or at the lawn in front of our house
and the huge white mushrooms that have grown there all summer, this morning
nothing but dull frozen lumps on the frozen ground. among the frozen dying leaves.
when you look at the angles of fieldrows driving the highways of
South Western Ontario, there is always that quick glimpse of a straight
empty row of dirt that reaches into the distance as it is replaced by another

        at the exact moment you saw it.

all the adventures we had had along the way, and as such they would be
 replaced by dreams, dreams and the occasional moment of speech.
the cornstalks we walked through to find the lights of fire trucks, all of us standing around
the fire. looking up we could not see the stars, although later
we could realize we were not really seeing. weird wonderful waking dreams
in which those rooms would actually fold up with us in them.

we were standing... somewhere...   pure magic
on fire with being, the Sunday afternoons of our lives. the trees,
their branches and their leaves, together they are the energy
of the world, waiting to be touched and then to fall away. the time
travel and such incarnations. it all becomes the earth waiting to catch us

        and hold us tenderly,

where memory becomes a solid of eternity.[21] for we were walking
along the side of the road when suddenly it struck us that we were
walking along the side of the road and it stopped us

        right in our tracks, stopped us all where we were...

✡ *Coda:*

wide open.   we are ready to embark into
imagine...   its is so nice to look there
(Our minds glass eyes and mist, youthful, on fire with being...)
boring the reader to death it was our duty
to watch the windows do whatever.   in the afternoon
there were many beautiful photo opportunities

between places and the sound   so still, what creates
a pattern in the human mind   and where am i?
at the exact moment you saw it   and hold us tenderly

right in our tracks, stopped us all where we were...

Endnotes

1 After some study, we decided that these trees were actually more highly developed forms of the local fungus, since they sprouted from the same rich soil that supported all the vegetation of that area. Earlier, we had discovered some particular soil that appeared to be composed of small mushrooms that clung to each other as they struggled to grow out of smaller fungi as they decomposed. The ecosystem was obviously growing and decomposing at the same time in these intricate layers of subtle colours we could not describe. Sometimes we counted as many as seventy-two new growths that managed to sprout from a single decomposition. Other times there were only two or three. Some specimens succeeded in growing as high as our ankles, but it was the trees that were truly magnificent, and it was around their stems that we could find the most interesting samples. When we stood perfectly still we could hear spore pods dropping through the moist air from the spread out canopy of the upper branches. Some round greenish pods we found were the size of tennis balls and we took turns throwing them at one of the thick stems poking up from the ground. They exploded like soap bubbles filled with smoke, the sort we had blown in the schoolyard as adolescents. They made a soft popping sound as they exploded in the windless air. When one of these powdery clouds hit the sunlight it created rainbows of deep ambers and purples, drifting slowly through the air until they came to rest quietly upon the brownish leaves scattering that landscape.

2 Childhood.

3 Often the dreams of trees will manifest themselves in various appendages, most often in the form of mushrooms and sometimes in the form of flying squirrels. Notice how certain mushrooms are found under certain trees. Their shapes will give you a clue as to what the tree in question may be dreaming about. (This is where we learned it.)

4 Fossil records have shown that the influence of so-called academia and institutionalized learning caused trees to have leaves that were as solid as the wood they lived upon. Trees simply had no idea of their own mortality, or cared not to acknowledge it. It was a time in which leaves had no desire to fall, nor did trees have any desire to lose them. Over time, however, with the introduction of human commerce, which began to flourish as early as the Cenozoic Era, trees learned that to ignore their own temporary forms was futile, for it was only their way of living in greed. They were witness to many other life-forms that became extinct, if not rendered completely tedious due to their strange belief in their immortality they were not capable of conquering. This is why we find such a difference between the skin (constant static) of mammals and the leaves (tempo-immortal consciousness) of modern trees.

5 It has been hypothesized in several well known papers that trees are quite aware of our fate as a species, perhaps more than we realize.

6 For some examples of tree poems, see the translations we have made that follow these notes.

7 See 'Appendages'.

8 There should be more slow noise (music) in the world. Record the sounds of trees for hours.

9 This, of course, is true for the trees of rural landscapes, where our studies took place. It has not been determined whether or not trees living in an urban setting experience the same kind of uphoria. We suspect, however, that a tree's environment has much to do with its state of mind.

10 Many human utopian political parties have been influenced by trees. See their shifting platforms, available in various fictional forms, for reference.

11 undercover all solstice long.

12 and as the leaves fall away it becomes so much easier to see through it all and into

13   as the leaves fall away it becomes so much easier to see through it all   into

14   as the leaves fall   it becomes so much easier to see   it all   into

15   as   leaves   it becomes so much easier to see   all   into

16   as   leaves   it   so much easier to see   into

17   leaves   so much   to see

18 and as the leaves fall away it becomes so much easier to see through it all and into

19 An anonymous piece of writing discovered one afternoon in October while dissecting the consciousness of a tree and meditating upon the concept of 'The Opening of The Field', the title of a book by the American poet Robert Duncan. There are many instances throughout the text that suggest it was written by Stokes.

20 The breath of clouds, as imitated by trees in earthly realms.

21 Seasonal Drift: .August contemplation of days, remember to slow down days again. October… days. they are, after all, only days: a surface clouds at three in the afternoon and a branch that suspends it (thought) shrink each single motions grows until it vanish into the perfectly capable blue (sea monster) (heaven) (wing gust) but it was the cool rain came down that time of year. nice, we thought, to close down the morning, the evening, and of now. (the end) to be the darkened skies of hold the holes of our dreams, all the excitement, all the lust, now is cool and heavy (closed) way down here in the just imagine what behind the clouds all our little veils falling from the trees come about their way to catch our little thoughts. we are all angels, all shy birds who watch each of us clouds out the front room window in the afternoon, from the inside out when we remember how we were absolute (happy) our dreams when they were our selves, shadows of branches at dawn.

Conwenna Stokes was born and raised in London, Ontario. She lives near Poplar Hill with her cat, Jonah. Her photographs, recordings and carvings are on display at the Forest City Gallery in London.

portrait of Conwenna Stokes by Alex Cameron

B'urd

Alex Cayce

COACH HOUSE BOOKS   TORONTO

The myth you were writing right now
is fine, though the plot needs a little work.

fix it. i dare you. nothing
but bursting tedium

out of the sky

could view life as an ongoing experiment
within the limitations of the flock itself
it offers several variations
upon a theme that can be directly
and intimately examined
because you are one of them living.

but could the world suddenly find a self
actively involved both mentally and physically
(wings are a shrinking structure) a language
singing of the immediate surroundings of soft air
instead of a viewed force
impossible to separate the drifting from the
poke and prod, prod and poke

that which uses hands (wings) and thinks
these things aren't attached to mind

    J.M.

🐦 Revolutionary Hymn (for the flocking birds)

life is not boring
            life is not tedious
if we woke up this morning we're probably alive

and all the sad fuckers
out there in the universe

      they don't even know how we died

We
      Don't
            Care

Four Small Birds Are

sitting twenty feet away watching me through the open window. Two rest in the dead oak behind the garage, two sit on telephone wires that lead to our house. If a sound or a sudden movement occurs in the atmosphere they burst apart, and I watch these quiet explosions knowing somehow those involved will always meet again. And they do. Sometimes they meet closer to me, then further away. Together, each of their weightless heads flit quickly, seemingly at the same instant, but then one shits upon the laundry Hazel hung out on the line to remind me they are only four small beings, each one living inside a little head, singing so alone, quietly beneath the soft breeze of their feathers. At the moment they have vanished, but they don't seem too far off; they never do. The sky gets so huge sometimes, and we the birds are so alone within it. The four again explode to what remains of the light, and I watch the feeder I hung last fall sway empty, and all of us remain outside, remembering this small unscheduled visit.

Morning Sky

Strange unpronounceable red outside
of the birds (Erik Satie was of
the birds, knew the plenitude of
clouds) wakes with a mysterious roar

the sun shoots out rays of red, orange,
blue and gold, and we are told our size,
somewhat larger than a squirrel
far less interesting than our own train

of thought speaks directly out of (time)
gathering a language no one tried to
learn (Erik Satie knew the lurch and
stretch of time) makes us so very small

just to wake us, just to make us small, 'we
lay at the bottom of a strange ocean, in bed
where the trees were pure sexual beings, swaying
in our heads and your breath was the smell

and Satie was the sound of the sky, slow
moving, promising whatever came to mind'

🐦 The Blue Sky Was Made To Float Against

Listen to me, the birds are here too, they have short, intense
lives, sparks of whyng-drift, a light shudder
AGAINST the light, and not in it. They will flyrt from
the innermost regions of any space or time into a
quantified moment of being alive, full of song (NOTHIN') a
language working in oppositions, present even when the body is not
(Present). Definitely the least threatening of all beings,
any species you like, Rose Breasted Grosbeak, Am-
Erican Redstart, the Killdeer, take your pick. It is
entirely worthwhile to pay attention, for if you only listen,
nothing but recognition of something invisible could be learned.

Listen to me, the feather was formed of light some time ago
in order that light might be carried thru the void. The Earth as
host for the migratory patterns of light. The bird, which is light,
comes from the egg, which is gravity. In turn, the egg comes from the
bird. As it is, things seem destined to move against their origin and
with it simultaneously. Such it is with the bird, and since we are
creations of imagination and continue to use it to destroy
itself, we should notice them, the birds, yes, we should, but
not because they are beautiful (and they ARE! THEY ARE SO BEAUTIFUL!)
But because thru them we might see to defy ourselves, yes, and the
intensity of that is a firm press upon the head, heart, hands, or genitals,
a soft tuft shyning, mixing consciousness, the full capacity of awareness
first thing in the morning and happy to be
that way uplighting whatever yr made of.

Sing where you come from and what you are in the space below.

Broken Wing

> 'A single specimen of the eastern tiger salamander
> reported for Point Pelee in 1915 has not been seen since that time'
> –Darryl Stewart (1977)

As you drive deeper into the album there is the distinct feeling
that something is coming apart, divided down the middle by the sound of it.

All that screaming only makes you want to drive faster, until the trees
are a blur of electricity. The effect is enough.

There is a gas station in a small town along the way, a beautiful girl
with black hair and fingernails who flies in
on a bicycle and fills your car with gas, the silence overwhelming, as
the wind and the universe

continue to collapse every second
you settle back into your dream of destination.

A casual disembowelment.
Headaches expand the soft skull to fill the driver's seat.
Aneurysm on the road. Annul that screaming.
The slight panic to keep them all awake.
There is no one in this place who will slit your wrists for you, so you drive
deeper into it awash in the white
blue sky.

Dream: (Destination

Where is it you want to go and will this recording take you there?
Where lyrics are sung by birds heard and not seen ever screaming
Screaming

Screaming Their Little Heads Off.
And the wind records each tiny extinction as the doorway opening upon the
	nature
of their tired thoughts

Nature the casual song
Mind the disruptive element

(In the dream you slowly begin to realize you have gone missing
as the parkland begins to unfold around you
the major life zones display their distinct lines, tired landmarks,
tired bones the size and shape of trees
merely convenient labels which blend smoothly into the recording.

Even at this point the sound of waves are invisible and you remember
that if the nature of song is to control, then this is where the album severs into
	melodic
undercurrents of sweetness and noise and the flora and fauna cannot exist
anywhere else
where you yourself cannot bother to pretend

Some Notes on Bird Songs

3) THE BIRTH OF LANGUAGE

The History of Language does not exist. However, it shall continue to be unborn at the exact moment that any member of the species comes into existence. How could you ever hope to study something you are? In the House of Language there are many who hope to speak with such purity and will talk into their graves.
Fly away now if your wings must be so heavy.

1) HOLOGRAMMATIC LANGUAGE

Language is holographic by nature. The written word is in fact the spoken word presented in a three-dimensional, spacial, format. Thus the wavelength of each letter used to make up a given word in its entirety is also the smallest 'slice' of that word necessary to recreate the hologrammatic image. The 'meaning' (stored memory, or learned information) appears to be stored ubiquitously throughout the cerebral matrix of language rather than in the interrelationship between the separate letters/notes. Language is the birth of hallucination. Flashcards to improve your writing. A clock in the shape of a dolphin. You should see the birds.

2) CHEMICAL LANGUAGE

As 'serotonin' enters your mind, it travels down the spinal chord, and enters the many wings of the body, at which time
                                                                                        comes to mind and hovers before thee,   hoping to open the twenty-six windows of perception in a seemingly random order. This is where a single spirit can rest on the larger, resulting windowsill of the mind, looking in two directions at once. Written to improve your flashcards. This dolphin should tell you the hours. You could be the birds.

4) EVOLUTIONARY LANGUAGE

mutation golare. (as it poens in th hoystri of th spiceis it connat be pecfert, thus it stum nad deos loces in th furtue [persnet, if sene form the pats] so much differently). who era th brids? flacshards era wrettin to tell th time. th livse of th dilphons are eras in nimd.

Fleye

8) TELEPATHIC LANGUAGE (INFINITE LANGUAGE)

7) ROMANTIC LANGUAGE

Because Language is the bridge between bodies, (a light swoop upon the air) that hoop which houses the mind, it is a bird house, whose sexual wings are perched upon those branches. It should be made clear that this language cares nothing for orientation, gender, age, species, or race. It is exactly what it is like to be with another person. If you call the right notes, someone is there who can answer

0) DEAD LANGUAGE[1]

In many archaic languages, the words for 'to not exist' are best translated into present day English as 'without the word' or

(see TELEPATHIC LANGUAGE)

6) FUTURE LANGUAGE

Time is the most difficult medium through which to communicate. This makes any attempt to predict their songs

A Short Review of Birds

Birds can be far more interesting than people sometimes. Today, in fact, as I pore over the lists of confirmed sightings I made years ago in the backwoods near Tilbury Ontario, birds seem less capable of an outright violent attack in any language. One simply remembers a shape among the leaves, and it is never the bird in its entirety, a thing in itself, but a suggestion, an attitude that leans toward the whole. Their unusual forms of communication always correspond directly to individual shapes, a series of objects open to interpretation instead of a defining mechanism through which facts are stated. They are a war with no violence, a peaceful tribe who carry out their discussions for the benefit of all without any attempt to triumph over their delicate presents. It is certainly a natural enough position, for the voice of a carnivore becomes as important as the voice of the small berry eaters. Thus no one is afraid to speak. It is comforting that each species can exist in order that it might be heard alongside all the others rather than against them, and similarly, that each song or cry made by any one creates a wildly varied universe in which everyone gathers in bunches separately causing an overall effect similar to that of a community of writers.

Lysdexia in Sunlight

what mournful singing
in the happiness of change: they
beat their drums across the cloud-lit skies;

by calling out our names
they are assured of an answer in their wingspan
a note quite high, (not sounded at all within that realm)

something you can hear uttered just in front
of the beak, to layer existence before the sound
itself appears, a priori, but so what:

their benign overwhelming attention
can only be explained by
Mind, not by the songs they sing.

After the Rain

After the rain the stink of the lake resides of the lake.
The good clean stink in the the back of my throat.

After the rain one can until anything can happen.
And stare at the wetback surface sit perfectly still.

When the glass of water becomes the glass of water.
The only think left to think:

After the rain nothing can ever sit quite through it.
When a bird goes so still as the sky.

'Gull sit on lake fine.
And it's after rain.'

After the rain no one's still day. Quite
so nowhere. It's a mind ever goes.

Even the rain felt straight down to strike the surface.
Ninety degrees of the lake.

🐦 Notes on Flight

here
love them because
here they are
not here

🐦

every being faces

many directions

with a face

to the sky

🐦

my wife sleeps
her head
the top of it
points up to
them hello
miles and miles
away

🐦

east night first
then western crackle (&
the greens become several shades
of blue, music obviously)
layered in the orange
orchid tufts going
to sleep

🐦

no moon
almost present
a sliver to speak
as it shares stars
with shapes and
shifters
the quiet
songs

cloudsex:
soft lightning
stroking the wet
gas light

feel them
moving in
the trees

jokes on you in the morning
when they aren't around it's you
who aren't so asleep or breathe in
the open eye WAKE UP

🐦

the feather cre
ates connexion
turbulence, a
worl(d)wind
the mind read
ily accepts
collage/com
pression in
time

🐦

mine breathe
you say yours can do anything, mine
mine breathe

🐦

if there are none look to the horizon
to see something of them, time held
on a refractory note until they gather
for you are inside the chest not the
head but in the chest where you are alive
look deep into their soft barricades

Float/Set

swimming at dusk, the water
feels like air, tho it cups the
balls more gently, holds them where

the careless gravity of the lake seems
to halt, and can float quietly, a
point of departure to wake up

those orange wisps and ochre folds
of cloud strings from across the water
that hang before the red sun wash and

that silence the lake is fumbling for
turns them into the circular motions
we make, both above and below the horizon

sound to hold our dark hovering limbs

Seasonal Drift

August contemplation of days, remember to
slow down days again. October… days.
they are, after all, only days: a surface

clouds at three in the afternoon
and a branch that suspends it (thought)
shrink each single motions grows until it

vanish into the perfectly capable blue
(sea monster) (heaven) (wing gust)
but it was the cool rain came down that

time of year. nice, we thought, to close
down the morning, the evening, and of now.
(the end) to be the darkened skies of

hold the holes of our dreams, all the
excitement, all the lust, now is cool and
heavy (closed) way down here in the

just imagine what behind the clouds

all our little veils falling from the trees
come about their way to catch our little
our thoughts. we are all angels, all

shy birds who watch each of us
clouds out the front room window in
the afternoon, from the inside out

when we remember how we were absolute
(happy) our dreams when they were our
selves, shadows of branches at dawn.

Flock

nothin's what it seems
lies, illusions, pure empty beings
together in nothing we are

in love with not being
here
        too

non-being slips over
into another wing
that's floatin' up the street eh?
away from the lake
into the what? a
fortress called forest

Leave Me Alone:

1 sound retreats forever into the wash

2 we have everything at every moment

3 the sound of the call is so pure

Birds Land on the Roof of This Room

and I am sad. They are so small and
I can hear the sound of their wings
folding as though there were no windows,
no wood, or air, between myself and them.
One roof over they squawk and shit
they hop about from feet to feet with
something great in mind, a terrific plan
to which I have not yet been introduced.
I listen to them surely discussing
the weather, what to eat, where to get laid,
etcetera. Then they fly off. I sip my coffee and
I am sad. Being human thinks so hard some
times of all the things we could have had.

🐦 Notes to an Untitled Poem

ONE) everyone please breathe to begin, for it is the air that holds us.

TWO) defined by a freedom to choose your voice, not to find it; to choose the chorus, not to discover any of them.

THREE) I still believe and will continue to believe we have much to learn from the flocking birds, those who move together and sing to each other. Unconcerned. Suspicious. Migratory and Feared.

FOR no real community could ever be fully understood as a community by anyone, even those who belong to it. FOR there should be such flexibility within the ranks. FOR the mystery of play we have gathered. FOR the presence of any ghosts you desire.

FIVE thru NINE) if involved in a community, however diversified or small, one tends not to feel a faceless stick in a group of empty sticks, as one does sitting on the subway during morning rush hour, then coming up the steps of St Andrew Station at say 8:28 in the morning, a herd of cattle oppressed to the extent of blindness and disregard. Where no muse could possibly bother to penetrate our sense of hopelessness. the death of the imagination first thing upon waking. but lives do exist in the sense that one finally feels free to exist as they may, in a complete and utter anarchy amongst the ranks, free breath for everyone! (breathe dammit) an intoxication in and about the premises that allows for this cast of invisible ballots that has real meaning.

TEN) it is the role of those already established to exploit all those interested in becoming a part of their community. despite how evil this may seem at first, it is for the benefit of the whole, since the older members will forever be comfortable in their declining years. Such 'exploitation', as it has been originally considered, will eventually wear away to something equivalent to mere initiation. Watch to see who shall fall far from the nest through our notes.

ELEVEN thru THIRTEEN) It might be said (indeed it shall) that I never really understood any sense of community until I met my inlaws, who are in fact humans of the divine order, an expansive family in many ways, limited in others, but for all intensive purposes are a flock of large birds, Canadian Geese or Whooping Cranes, travelling among each other across a sky no one else will ever see. I would naturally come to understand them first, for they have been doing what all other communities I encountered set out to do without saying a thing. And while strife may occur among them, it is because they actually feel that way about some other person, and not because of some theoretical fakery caused by their own sense of failure, or because they are unable to accept the fact that things could easily be otherwise. A GREAT BLUE HERON FLIES OVER THE 401. What could be more beautiful?

FOURTEEN) history is the vehicle of the community, tradition the forgetting thereof, and the intensity of any layer will resonate against the intensity of all others at any given moment until the high note of the underworld commune breaks through. Watch us shift together to flock across your sky.

FIFTEEN) a community of losers such as sparrows, pigeons, or european starlings, all of them surviving on the crumbs of the establishment, are outsiders within the wings. they tend to be more open minded, more diverse and revolutionary; they have more will to sacrifice. It has been said it is wrong to bite the hand that feeds you but there are only so many ways to survive, and what if those hands have never offered anything let alone a meal? Flesh is food too, as is the mind. Consider the pigeons. Bite away! Will you never be cared for by those who have agreed that culture should be raped and pillaged for their own security? When will thanks be given for what has been given? The Real Planet lives in an atmosphere of doubt. At least someone can think about how the real planet is dying. At least some think about it differently.

Bravery must be Stupidity, but hopefully it will survive.

Endnotes

1 Such as it is, ORIGIN is a tricky phenomenon to negotiate, let alone come to terms with. It is your gift to be present precisely where you are not.

Alex Cayce lives in Windsor Ontario, where he is a member of The South Western Coalition for the Birds. His wife Alice is an artist, specializing in water colour and sketch. Her work often accompanies each of these texts. She has had exhibitions at the Jack Miner Bird Sanctuary and at the Point Pelee National Park Recreation Centre.

portrait of Alex Cayce by Alex Cameron

heartrants

H. Azel

COACH HOUSE BOOKS   TORONTO

If you have never thought there was
a hope for yourself as a writer
or artist or human being
it only makes sense to help someone else
who might escape your fate.

writing with other names or beings
builds the emotions at all times
for whom you are a release mechanism.

greetings, hello, love is real
erotic as the banal

'Jay MillAr says fuck you
she loves you all anyway.'

greetings to these loves
you are & have been
quite like living with all this other
AS A PERSON IN A SHELL
i appreciate your various
attempts to spell the real for me

    J.M.

ONTARIO[1]

The largest country I ever encountered is Ontario. Its many regions stretch from coast to coast, and I must admit, are rather pleasant to travel through. Each one of them have something special to offer. I must recommend to any one capable of travel: you must lift your feet up and make the effect real! However, be reminded that there is only so much of the mind to experience across any countryside. You cannot go anywhere in this place without seeing all the beautiful women. Women walking, women smoking cigarettes, women talking on the phone, women riding their bicycles, women writing letters, women dancing. They make deals, go to work, take showers, attend parties (there are naked women all over the place wearing clothing, women who fall asleep in cars, laughing women, women wearing pants and sweaters). Here women write novels in their heads; there are women who speak out loud to cats. Sometimes the women cry. It is very lovely to see, but sad, too, in a way no one will never understand. These are just some of the women in our country. They are everywhere and they Keep Ontario Beautiful.

Travelling Through the Algonquin

As the moose crossed the road, she turned her head
sleepily, watching the two of us with soft dark eyes. It was
then that I witnessed one of the shapes of my love for you,
not in the moose itself, but seeing how we were to travel
much deeper into the Algonquin and into each other for that
whole week. The entire world was present, something to travel
around us and in us, and we would wake to discover we were in
it together, making it all happen. As we walk along this road
we listen to frogsongs, and it's as though we are shielded from all
sound by an invisible bubble. Everything becomes more and
more distant the closer we become. The music of the loons,
however, passed directly through us, piercing our other,
inner selves upon a tawny fox peering at us from atop this
stone embankment, carrying us away as we glide by at a
quiet speed, invisible and indivisible to everything around

❧ Notes Toward a Poem on Our Honeymoon

There are no details of the honeymoon I will ever
offer in any public space.

                                These are to remain buried on
that fine line somewhere balanced between my consciousness
and my subconsciousness as a recurring erotic dream, separate
entirely from the world others inhabit, but entirely a part of
our own. However, there was one day that we emerged
from our cabin recluse and drove to Pembroke Ontario and walked
up and down the main street looking at the small but human
people sitting in the restaurants and cafes. Later, sitting among
them in a diner called 'Cafe Guy', we looked out the front
window and across and up the street into a parking lot where a small
twister was twisting, picking up dust and swirling it around in
such a way it appeared to be two ghost-like bodies spinning
together, wrapping themselves into one. Then it snapped, and
was gone

Jewel

to escape with you is my imagination

How hard is it to open up the heart all the way? I often see the oblong rolling case of time distancing itself, lengthening through my solitary work as a writer, but then to see someone walk into the wind of it, that is altogether a human vehicle. Consider, for instance, the landscape of the north. We found movement possible there, an entire breath into a cavity where we are most alive. There are so many lonely places where death is always a factor, but in the northern regions, of which there are many, there is a calm sense of openness, an empty disregard for any of the closed human systems we have to choose from. It is a landscape of possibility, which makes it unhuman, and therefore easier to fill with what is human. These arms can reach wherever they are for those roads we have travelled into the light without any fear of the speed it presents et cetera. I am never really present in these southern places of entropy and despair, because of the knowledge I have of escape. And I have actually discovered no documentation of them in the literature. However, it is the story of my life (fear) that leads me (mind) back here (afraid) because there is always the possibility that I will never see them again. But as long as there are places to go while we are here death cannot exist. So I shall invite you to relive it now.

> JOURNAL ENTRY, NOVEMBER 2396. *Living in the Ottawa Valley this year was incredible. On our first day there we climbed to the top of the hill and looked, and it was no more than an observation of what we could be as ordinary onlookers. As the wind came up over the trees there was suddenly no need for the imagination (escape) as we had needed in the city. Here it was in any part of the sky. Our tents rested under huge pines that stood beneath the misshapen clouds all summer, stood there until the deciduous began to turn. And they were ours, and we lived in them. I remember the levels of spaciousness and warmth were so huge, lying across the sky and the land, something untouchable, for we were inside what had been built for us by ourselves, through whose air the leaves are now falling sadly (becoming birds), as we make our way back to the city. Everything we heard we will remember as the voice of a time which the mind sees while we wondered what was happening before there was such a thing as thought. Sometimes I can still hear them.*

I remember being the soft dirt of an unused path in the middle of the forest for two weeks. When I returned to our camp I allowed language to take the shape of a mythology that reminisced in the youthful juvenation of anyone who would listen, but only in soft green leafiness beneath the many layers of trees, and in two woodpeckers whose sound was similar to that of fire. Who had the only ears then, and in what space was the reason to fear anything at all? ((no fear) (crimson tents) (one sky)). It was by far the best death I have ever experienced, or woke to. Who really needs to be alive there was the topic for which we searched out any answer in a physical experience: a peculiar lesson directed at the empty trees surrounding our departure.

> FROM A LETTER, JULY 2389. *Dear you, can I ease your bones by saying that we rented a cottage on Manitoulin Island that August and did nothing of any importance to the world? We certainly enjoyed the mornings when we rose to eat local mushrooms gathered along the shore of the lake. There will come a day when we shall find a dead tree and sit upon it, having already gathered the necessary waters into our aprons. But it is dew we seek, not water, and therefore it shall be that much sweeter to the touch when we find it.*

Eventually everything becomes how we can take the time to make love at odd hours. If we talk it becomes spirit, and we are real ghosts all the time because we can still remember what it was like to be alive. But will we ever know exactly how the past contracts and how the future expands to its full capacity within our heads? With the future present like that there can be no extinction.

> JOURNAL ENTRY, AUGUST 397. *One night we woke to discover that all the water was instead rock, and that the road was something that naturally had no end, no matter how much we longed for it. We decided we should sleep in the safe shape of the car with the rock everywhere around us, even in our dreams under the surface of the cloudless sky. We dreamt of swatches of conifer that noiselessly parried the wind along the highest evelation of road possible in this country. And my legs fell asleep. I had to get out of the car to walk it off (darkness) (station wagon) (the stars ring) high as a kite at the side of the empty road, and the whole night was alive, swarming with your sleep there. Eventually, we never made it to the Mecca of Timmins. We were going to Timmins for a wedding.*

I am trying to open up my heart, but I bite my nails instead. Is it true that I have been somewhere and longed for you in the night? Your body is forever a landscape I am both familiar with and foreign to. Because it is not mine. But if I turn to face the north you are there because perhaps you are thinking about it too. You are so absolute you become perception. Watching you turns on the tactile scope for hours, a whole province, perceptive as anyone could hope to be, and Alive, What A Creature, the title of a yet unwritten poem. The purest scent of your heart is trapped by all wildlife: small woodland creatures and gentle carnivorous beasts who know exactly how to kill; plantlife such as the maple or the pine, dandelions, tulips, and bulbous root-like beings. When I witness them in their natural environment I believe I shall finally give in to the soft light and hope found in your voice or your body. And there shall be a language you have not spoken, bits of memory carried by all these creatures we have shared together or apart. In the sound of no one can tell me any other story.

> JOURNAL ENTRY, SEPTEMBER 597. *The day became so dark after the sun set, but only because we saw it falling from the beach. On the other side of the island across the bay the trees would see it disappear long after we did, in a precise manner, and we would never know their exquisite perspective as we wandered along the darkness of a road through the forest. Birds and cicadas, in fact any sound that was emitted by the forest, their technology was so frightening in the dark, for they offer keys to the possibilities we are programmed to imagine, and the overall response is terrifying, a small point aware of itself in the middle of nowhere, searching for something familiar in the outer realms of a single fading beam. We held each other's hand. It was that easy.*

Dear voice of the heartland, hello. I shall be living here to fall into you like a stone skipped across a northern lake, so still it never stops fluttering like quiet birds skimming for insects. Loons and swallows, trout and lamplight, photographs of you against all the scenery I have ever seen. A quick taste and back into the air of my self. How should I float but across skin until my heart melts? With no desire just the brilliant fucking core?

Dear body of the headland, hello. I will wear you like the cool breath of the photographs we took last summer in Northern Ontario. With them you build me a forest and call it by your name, each leaf another reason to speak your name, slightly animal, each branch another dream. As you build me your fortress and call it by your name build me a fortress build me a fortress buildme a fortress and I will live there with you in the shade of the shade, our tent resting exactly where we placed it. It is so human to move into an empty space that way, to make it familiar by our touch.

> JOURNAL ENTRY, WINTER SOLSTICE, 97. *When we stand still we point to the north. By sitting or lying down we face many directions at once. We should remember this is ever we find we are lost.*

When I think of holding you, (either against skin or in visions), my mind goes places, and the weather is never against us there, no matter what it may be. Here the elements of the world are alive (breath). All the places I have ever been are nothing without the elements, but you, with your milky face in the sky over our northern landscape, you open to where I stand here on some path and think of you. You are always either just ahead or behind. It is always so early in the morning, and in the beginning of this day the green explodes, waiting for the evening when the sun is a ghost tree, shining against it all.

> A NOTE TACKED TO THE DOOR: *I am looking inside where you always are and where hope continues to be.*

Toronto, 2002.

19A (97)

if I were other than I am
it could only be because I was then.

That I never entirely fell in love with the human planet
as it has been presented is not my fault. But I love you.

In looking behind, that past expands in such a way
as to make this the rotting fruit of just having lived.

Just something else to deal with. And time is such a fucking useless medium
through which to communicate. However, the knowledge

of such things couldn't possibly help. This is a poem
now, not when the past might have speeched for itself.

If I was not who I have become
it is because I was not ever then.

It is the age between things that can never be removed. We
forget we are either an age forever or we never were.

We get so tired
feeling something lost

this vision always begins with the road rolling over the foothills
towards the Rockies, or along a road that leads thru the mountains themselves,
then curiously shifts to every other place that could possibly be
sometimes you are present sometimes you are not
the sun is always setting and the appearance of them all against the sky
is at an angle always appreciated by

and never actually leaving them, mind always the being present
as though you couldn't possibly imagine an existance beyond
this note, this second, or these legs crossed
over one another in the back seat, young enough to know
death has no ability to respond to the nobility
of such an age growing outwardly suddenly

as dad drives silently all colour anihlates the emotions,
sitting there, 70 km/hr, thinking nothing in the boredom of driving
without sound or expression. The breeze of an open window rides
cool against that skin, this thing remembered later as only an illusion can be,
somewhere your mind went once momentarily and shared a brief
tilt with the universe

and afterward, it's either rock or tree, stone or wood or words
and earth, and words

19c (97)

yes, everyone WILL
exactly as they please.

everyone is so
outside

it has driven us crazy the pity for years and years

everyone is so out there
trapped in it all

'Relax, the time
has not yet come.
They will behave
exactly as they have
trained for years
to become. We
are still in training.'

My Dear, please restart the page.

*My Dear, please try to
consider the past as a phenomenological study of the present.
Suck on the pit until you are high. Until the heart, squeezed
to a coal-like blossoming under the weight of all you will ever
experience, lifts, and flowers into the neck, feet, or hands.
But never the head. Don't worry. Your head is safe.
Never ever in the head. Eventually, however, the past will
sour like bored milk, and the graceful arbitrary motion of the
day will come forward, almost sexually, in fact. Consider it
a leaf pierced upon the end of a stick, turning blue, and it will
become coated with layer upon layer of silky moss until the
origin of the actual is hard to make out precisely. Turning
away the last possible thought about it. The future is so empty
in order to build the mystery. It only makes up for the lack of interest
that has ever occurred. Because I can see you there*

❧ Two Adventure Stories Not Necessarily in That Order

PART ONE(?)
An Adventure Story Involving the Unification of All Things

Three hours later, after trying to sleep, I was in my car driving back across South Western Ontario. It was quite a stay, filled with overwhelming highs and lows, and it was troubling now that I could not seem to find an even thought on which to stand. During my drive I would occasionally take a glance upward through the bug-bespeckled windshield at a sky that held itself over the flat, dry landscape of that region, and it didn't quite appear to be the sky any more, although I was positive it was a sky: a perfectly flat sky from which the clouds hung and billowed back and forth. And the closer I came to you, the source of my actions, the more flat and blue and white the sky became, while the clouds thereof grew more and more dynamic, and golden, so that by the time I stopped there was no natural religion, there was no human religion, yet I knew that everywhere I look will be forever filled with what is not there. What a risk in that small chance of someone experiencing both sides of their mind at once! I thought it just may be a kind of exquisite sweetness I could not possibly hope to explain, but somehow know that to taste of it is to love; love of fins, breath and skin, feathers, of stone, of eyes, the shell and speech, of skulls and sheet metal, of mouth, petals, ears, of you. How peaceful is the unnaturally thoughtful space of your body! how it fits and how it is my job to find it again and again amongst the confused, broken ruins of our perfect world. And it was made clear to me that day, at the end of my adventure as I walked through the sunken doorway of our home to find you standing at the sink washing the fragile blue dishes from which we would eat, that all things, no matter how great or small the distances between them, begin in you.

PART TWO(?)
An Adventure Story Involving the Separation of All Things

The adventure that had landed me in Point Pelee National Park at seven o'clock on a Sunday morning had been to that minute unexplainable, but finally all the pieces of my consciousness were falling into place. And it was as night speared itself upon the sun that I met the red-winged blackbirds and the cool blue-black swallows with their warbled introductions. There were big blue carp to greet as they bubbled around us, and the occasional moss-green snapping turtle. A single great blue heron, standing as the rest of us sat around together making noise. It was all very much like an attempt on behalf of my species to meet other species at a great conference that, at least on our part, had been poorly advertised. But after watching the yellow flowers of the lily pad actually opening slowly to the morning sun I became certain that all of that world, normally thought of by our species as natural, could no longer be anything other than a collective of motion. Suddenly I was tired and hungry, exhausted in fact, and so I drove into Leamington and went to a tiny, broken down restaurant where I sat among fellow human creatures who, like me, were eating the most disgusting breakfast I have ever seen. And listening to all the useless noise gathered around me like so much flesh coloured play-dough I could not eat, nor could I look at those present. All of which did nothing to ease any of my previous suspicions: that we are all senseless and stupid and there must be a pure form of human intelligence lying elsewhere in the world, somewhere where it is not necessary. As we left the restaurant I couldn't remember having felt so confused or alone, knowing I would soon be travelling Across South Western Ontario and away from the secrets of a balanced world without thought.

Or

Or the wind covers so much ground and won't even think of you. High wind, White sky. Or you miss it and close the window. Think of the cicadas and the beer. The middle of August. Or you don't even notice. Driving Across South Western Ontario. Or the open sky along the trees like a door. Or the doorway and the windowsill and the wind. Waiting for the cicadas who are not there. Remember the front porch, the two of us. Thinking. Or the breeze through the leaves. Or today thinks about becoming night. Hot, lazy, breezy and loud. Or you open the window against the flimsy crickets making the sky red. five minutes. Driving Across South Western Ontario. Or remember the cicadas at four in the morning in Windsor Ontario. Or remember the cicadas in the afternoon in Toronto Ontario. The sound of a guitar, the voice that goes with it. Talking with the wind. Or you think of the cicadas in Windsor Ontario and drive. Hear the flimsy crickets. Or the wind. Or You Point To The Sky. Driving Across South Western Ontario. You think and it's there. Or the sweat on your back. Or the heavenly traffic. The swish of the cars, this engine's rattle. Or the wind finds you and you think it cares. Awake at dawn in the basement. Or was it dawn talking. We were talking, couldn't see it was light. Falling asleep and the music. Or you tumble down the past. five years. Perhaps there was a pattern inherent all that time. Or the cigarettes and the beer. The smoke and the pattern. Driving Across South Western Ontario. Just imagine the cicadas and the crickets in Lucan Ontario. Or the clouds that were in the sky for breakfast on the patio. All the clear white near the horizon in Windsor Ontario. Tired and hungry. Stiff back, high country. Or nothing but a cup of coffee. The things that have just never been said until now. Or we pause for a moment and 125 km/hr. Somewhere in Ontario. The music might make you cry. The simple guitar and the voice. Driving Across South Western Ontario.

❧ A Report to the Revolutionaries of That Period[2]

For a world once filled with such modern [*unreadable*] it was certainly became void of any feeling. This was our interpretation of this strange place. Years we spent there, and in the urban centres that remained standing for all that time we noticed that those bodies severed at the neck did not smile. Not that the head was actually missing, but that it was never put to [*unreadable*]. We should know. We were there. Our humble [*unreadable*] were constantly picking up strange frequencies. We discovered through the close study of arbitrary documents the species is famed for that these were some of the many areas that had been nicely [*word unknown*] in the past and were now lost forever, only to be minutely heard with the correct equipment – But why this one parasite in particular, referred to in subsequent reports as the [*word unknown*], grows as it does across the species, its source located in the [*word unknown*], and how, or why, everything comes to it by the strange habit of [*word unknown*] the fourth dimension, turning the very moments of the day into the solidity of a commodity, remains one of the culture's greatest [*unreadable*]. For in their youth they had ideas, and they lived by them. Perhaps in the years to come, as [*word unknown*] learns the better of itself, all will be becoming as we once were, and will return to a [*word unknown*] notion of time. But now, deep within the various experiments of the present that have been [*unreadable*], many of our observers have returned somewhat affected, as though this buzz persists and amplifies wherever it can, and we are now left wondering if perhaps [*unreadable*] we missed the point, as it were, living so deeply in our forts of love and [*The remainder of this document was not readable.*]

Why Do They Call it a Towel

i never actually wanted to know what it was i was eating but every one was always so insistent on telling me to stand up straight, mind your manners, look both ways and then cross on that fine line between anything you could make your mind up to walk along, be completely suspicious and terrified of everything around you, dark green shit in the toilet, it's a rainy day in June and life is sweet and sour, something is rotting in the garbage can so i have to spend five minutes cleaning it out, there are all these moments that pass and pass along a little message, and then it's clean and everything continues, when i left the reading the other night i was followed out by the scraping footsteps of a lonely poet, drunk enough to be called a heckler, led away after asking one of the readers 'What Do You Know?' William said 'They're kicking him out because he never published a real book,' but he stood off to the side, looking over his shoulder and trying to maintain his balance at the same time, when i left Bob was attempting to read something, i walked past the heckler who flat out asked me with great concern 'Where's the projection of the poem?' and i had to agree i couldn't find it either, he followed me out scraping his feet like a very demon behind me and i broke out into laughter, there are all these moments that pass and pass along a little message, who are all these people and what are they doing here? walking along Bloor street today the air was all around me, cool but humid, making my shirt stick to my skin and my skin to the meat that's sticking to my bones, why is it that i am the only one that's dying while everyone else just continues to rise, we all smoke dope, we're all perverted, we all long for the tall cool frothy peace of death in our own pathetic lonely ways, we all want to take it on like an afternoon nap, a nightcap in the morning, we are all cowards, ignoring the inevitable in interesting ways, all these moments that pass and pass along a little message, the library was closed but i got to talk with this guy named Skye, named after the island where i thought maybe he had been conceived, who was sitting on the steps eating a triple decker peanut butter sandwich and telling everyone who dared to walk up the steps that the library was CLO-OSED, and he told me his philosophy of life which is, and i quote: 'I'm 34, I guess I'd better start thinking about an RRSP because unemployment can only go so far, that guy Mike Harris, he's an asshole,' and i don't tell him that even tho Harris is a complete prick i don't think he's all bad since he is causing a kafuffle, something that might be good for Canadians at this point in our career, and Skye meanwhile is heavily troubled by science fiction, it makes him as 'what if?' too many times about any given situation, there are all these moments that pass and pass along a little message, and walking home i discover in an alley an entire collection of Russian music waiting for the trash and the kids hanging outside the men's club waiting for their fathers to finish their beer waiting for the game to end help me pick out which ones to take with me, 'Take that one', the boy with the purple stains at the corners of his mouth says, 'I made that', the cover of the album is purple with half a treble clef on it, it's called *USSR Bolshoi Theatre* and he says 'I made that', and i believe him, i pick out seven or eight records and get up to leave and the oldest kid there says 'Hey, why's he takin the CDs' and i explain to him that someone left them in the alley for me to find, some gentle soul who wants me to explore the music of the four corners of the earth, and i can see right away that he doesn't believe me so i ask him if they're his and he looks dumbfounded, he's playing a hand-held Nintendo game and i can tell he wants to get back to his game, so i ask him if he knows who's records they are and he shrugs his shoulders and turns back to his game and i walk off, there are all these moments that pass and pass along a little message, and i come home and start to write a little poem about the other morning when i was getting out of the shower thinking about how sweet life is when everything is wet and i asked you 'why do they call it a towel?' and you said you didn't know and you were beautiful, beautiful as the tiny soprano voice on the purple record the kid had made peeling out that high beautiful note that hangs on the air in so many innocent ways, making me think there are all these moments that pass and pass along a little message

❧ *I came to be where I was 5 minutes ago*

The first thing I ever tried to learn was how
unfolding as I began to write without fear or knowing what next
The Pail and the Shovel. An idea continued to perform outwardly
for hate, for revenge, because these were the things that happened.
it had become clear thro the ages, anything was permitted to be
Red Sunset over The Lake. A Tree Broken of Leaves. The Beach

Which is Now. And there were those who dried out
looked at from the side, a Space in which each poem is perfectly
it becomes a poem, nothing more. And still you were running
looping into themselves to catch the little mayflies in their beaks,
I am thankful it is your light, my eye, and all of that

❧ *5 minutes ago where I was I came to be*

Recognising that there was the ridiculous nature of being
'Pale grey horse of the abattoir, rising'. For this was the mark,
the many tricks like a trained gull. Hovering for glory, for love,
And we let them happen, for we were living in a time, when, as
written across a sky of such blank air. As Long As It Was There.
And The Cool Water. There You Go, running as if you had wings.

To follow those one-eyed pigeons of that notion. Literature
chiselled, perfectly sounded and polished still High Buff: from
an idea across the sand, until you stopped to see the swallows
Light As Air the Snap and Swallow. And for that, my love,
with which to see.

❦ *Critique of the Living*

There have always been
five things in a row:
      footprints, or to speak of
whatever happens
at any free moment:
      feet first

            _____ ,

'_____ ,   _____ ;'   (SPEECH)

        _____ ,

  _____ ,

The second takes on five things of its own

Other times the third is
away if it grows bored.
Is time pure reason?: think;

Think the fifth shy stick upon which
birds sit in the present, singing of what is
happening in that moment

'Each day the five, present
after the other, grow into
his eyes to find row after row
of the mental creature
one who moves along
in sneakers, until I finally reach
about where I am in the world
that repeats after yesterday in
changes are subtle, finding out
where I was yesterday, or
tomorrow, where ever one
can see above their many heads.'

And I might wake with a start :
    the morning. And, to boot,
in such a way that some
    become something new.

꧁ Critique of the Dying

Of the fingers, or
to find itself being meditated upon, great Death
of the day, held or otherwise

these various forms. Sometimes it has
other times it is translucent
but takes its own time to walk up and down

And it grows bored. That fourth
quite rare moment, a shy
time lingers on and sings.

prepare the self for one
mental creature who has opened
two windows, and here are discoveries

designated to be alive at this time.
Building quietly in a green shirt,
what amount of understanding could be

rearing itself in today? Alive,
here to notice that the
not that much different from

will be tomorrow. And I will be
another sky of rare
things retreating in that order.

Something to do will be again in
always disappear

(They may actually change
be content in what I do.)

His Face Looked Like Satie
Sounds

Max could lie there for hours
near the fireplace, then jump aside
sideways and become someone else's
dog for the rest of the afternoon.
Sometimes I liked it when he was
my dog, other times I like to pretend
I was borrowing him from the neighbours.
During the winter we'd go running
together through the night air around the
block and I would run as fast as I could
with him running the same speed,
just ahead of me, and I would fall
to the ground and let him pull me
across the ice and snow by his leash.
Sometimes I could slide 30, 40 feet.
It was a stupid thing to do. Maybe
I could have broke his neck, but he
never complained or let out a yelp or
anything. When we stopped moving
he would always come back and sniff
at me, making sure that I fell down
because I wanted to. I knew lying
there in the flat silence of winter that
he liked making sure I was okay. One
time his leash snapped, but I said
he'd pulled too hard, excited by some
bitch. He was a little crazy and we
all knew it was possible. By 1990
my parents realized that Max was a
farm dog, so we moved to the country.
Max was happy there, and he roamed

about without the confusion of the
maze-like suburban landscape he
grew up in. It fit his brain better,
and as his brain grew to a comfortable
dog size, he kept to himself, running
and running around the back wood
lot, sniffing at everything to make
sure it was all okay, until he came
home one afternoon in 1992 limping
and shaking, covered with mud and
blood. Looking embarrased that
the pack of stray dogs had gotten
the better of him down by the creek
again. And that night he died. It's the
look on his face I hallucinate from time
to time, at moments of flat stillness
against the light, a look somewhere
between pain and shame, his head hung
low as he comes in through the screen
door at the back of the kitchen, shaking
and amazed that all those assholes had
been allowed into the world. We buried
him in the back yard, just north of the
garden, and Mom cried even tho she's
a toughie, so I tried (after looking into
her soft eyes) to justify it all by thinking
youthfully of how Max was now free to run
as he pleased, Dog Of The Four Winds,
a great sniffing spirit. But as I thought
this he just lay there in a black garbage bag
as dad shovelled the dirt back on top.

Postscript:
Today, new years day, 1997, there is someone
pulling me across the cold ice of the world,
and today I share his amazement.

❦ In Another Shimmering Lifetime

(an attempt at memory for you)
January 1390

1   Picture everyone there loving strangers, met only a few months earlier, their various shapes friendly, filled with chatter. Each of them easily a non-threatening member of an anonymous group of people that did exist once, during the patch-work lifetime of someone who could make their acquaintance and disappear soon enough. In the dark living room, a television flashes dull bluish streaks across bodies and brown bottles; quiet sentences are heard as they pass back and forth between people. Through the doorway to the kitchen a bright land can be seen, where voices climb, and never dare to fall. In that blaze I can see my father sitting around the wooden table with his voice. Those sitting at the table are welcome inside the sound of it, not only as pieces of the discussion, but as a source for the gentle interplay of mind. A space is present there, where youth has forged a middle-aged being out of challenge and intrigue, a mind that appears to be enjoying his quick rallies, a kind of professing sage, drinking beers like the rest them, a man who has looked behind himself through those present before him, who has suddenly found himself back at university, this time at the actual pinnacle of a conversation from the vantage point of his own future. My attention is back in the living room where laughter suddenly jumps up and heads for the washroom. Two girls sit cross-legged in front of the television. One of them giggles and a flower blooms, from the top of her head, and begins to shine in purples, yellows, and in the attempt to hold all of my attention, but wilts away when the five guys sitting across the couch, each one on their fourth or fifth beer, laugh at a joke about her ass she does not hear. There are others in the room too, figures who are coated in shadow, mysterious beings who at this moment are further away from my mind, ghosts whose voices can be heard warbling over the television like this seven year-old tape recording of themselves. And the colours there, in that room, grow mouse-like with each stupid gesture, each one a tiny scampering of emotion and fear.

2   Looking into the kitchen my father has vanished.
Outside he is building a bonfire in a snowdrift.
We all crowd the window, amazed at this, totally our discovery,
and as we admit the novelty of this moment,
we throw on coats and boots and head out in search of light.

Merry once again, finally, and in our drunkenness
we have become wholly unconsciously blind to the ugly possibilities of the season.
This is the whole night, what it became in the years to come.
In the future, which is part man, part woman,
there will always be this rage against our darker emotions,
against the cold nature we all come to know as human beings.

A goof-ball escapade of youth trapped forever in the shimmering air,
close to the nostrils and the mouth and the eyes, giving warmth.
This feeling finally solidified around midnight,
as the soccer match exploded into the empty luminescence of the cornfield,
under the mothball light of a full moon; and the girls
choosing to remain huddled near the fire talked about it,
choosing to ignore the drunken shouts of boys
kicking at the black and white ball dad produced from the garage,
aiming each shot between makeshift oil-drum goal posts to the east and to the west,
they talked about it in whispers.

On the field there are the sounds of crunching snow and crazy laughter,
they plow into each other for hours, not even keeping score; around the fire
there can be heard the quiet warmth of the fire glow,
as it licks at their feet, in praise of the night,
that which knows the soft heady warmth of morning,
and the remembrance of dreams.

And between these places I have travelled in one night,
and at each point that I remained still I was one of the people of that place.

(2.5)

(Dad stands near the fire talking and grinning,
he is watching the soccer game with his back to the fire,
he will throw on a log or two to keep it going,
the same way he has all night long
throwing matter into our minds for us to use.)

3   And the soccer game was suddenly a stupid ball
caught in a momentum directed either to the east or the west,

without purpose or resolve, finally to stand in someone's footprint marker.
And the fire to which we returned was cheery, but tiring to look at,

and it slowed us down, somehow, and the night grew suddenly lonely and apart
and the heaviness of the air came to sit upon our breath.

And cars began to disappear from the driveway.
And Dad said goodnight and went into the house to bed.

And we had to coax someone from the bushes,
reassuring him that she had not been overly embarrassed by his actions.

And afterward, to let everyone know he was fine, he tackled me,
diving over one of the blue and white oil drums in the dark blur of memory,

knocking the wind out of me for five long minutes.
And the colours of the night began quietly to recede then,

as I lay there near the fire, in the white darkness of the snow.
Feel the teenage rush of it all again receding, under the snowball moon,

a groaning beneath the dark sway of the pines.
And my breath will hang for all time, like grey angels or tiny stars,

in my mind or the black sky;
there.

Endnotes

1 There are so many women in our country blissfully unaware of how beautiful they are. Please be aware she makes all of you beautiful even if you don't want to be.

2 One could look towards and learn from the popular engravers of that period. Their methods by which to remove so many of the unnecessary layers, or by which to fruitfully ignore them, were not only ingenious, but easily imitative. Sadly, these have been lost to the world forever.

'I have met at least nine incarnations of my wife to date, and I have to admit that each one of them has been incredibly patient while the drunken orangutan was writing, but you should see all of them walk into a room together, no one on this planet could hope to write like that.'

– from *H. Azel's Dream*, Book Thug 1999

portrait of H. Azel by Alex Cameron

Perfectly Ordinary Dreams

James Llar

COACH HOUSE BOOKS   TORONTO

I always wanted someone to follow me around
from day to day who could write down my
dreams so i could look at them from
outside myself like flowers or
teapots or clouds. my regards to the fiction of the
moment, you are the sweetest being i ever knew,
a tall blonde colour'd shadow,
biographer of all the moments i wasn't
paying attention to my own mind.
Not Possible.
how could i possibly hope to
disregard my own mind?
i'm sorry you get all the credit and no one
understands your poems. but thanks to you
i now have more time
to consider the artwork of the clouds.
    J.M.

Prelude to a Perfectly Ordinary Dream

lying in bed this morning
light start wakes the window
all present so it might hold the sight of the blood
to see it pulse her neck is to see
how the skin jumps
absolutely alive in the memory
these dreams

every morning we stopped at the same restaurant for breakfast
the same restaurant somewhere in the midwest
until we knew we weren't going anywhere
driving a day at a time and arriving at the same place we left
though the restaurant became a little more chaotic each morning
not so it was uncomfortable, but so we could take the time to notice
waitresses smashing into each other, flocks of dishes flying,
one morning the cash register fell over and exploded
random swizzle sticks from the bar shot randomly
through the necks of people as they attempted to bite
their raw bacon sandwiches
we always ordered the same thing, ham and eggs,
it was terrible, boring placenta and rubber tar,
as though we were desperately hoping each day would move
to a perfected level of chaos and since the world
around us seemed destined to remain exactly the same
but fall to pieces and us in the middle
it was ridiculous, the calm bite on a fork that could not
bother to complain about infinite possibilities
but about food instead
every day we left a smaller tip
not because the service was bad
we were growing more and more concerned
about the monetary value of things
where we were heading

back in this light there comes a sigh
a bodily shift to the blood a little faster

⊕ *Perfectly Ordinary Dream #0 (March 19, 1992)*

I met my wife in a photograph my father showed me.
In it I am wearing full 1920s speakeasy regalia,
complete with Doc Martens for the futuristic effect that was
popular at the time, my trousers rolled up at the bottom,
my hands in the pockets of my jacket
and a green scarf around my neck.
I face the camera with a broad grin.
My wife is standing three or four feet away,
turn'd sideways. (It is a landscape photo,
taken on our trip to the mountains, none of which,
amazingly, and thankfully, can be seen.
The colours of the sky in the background are recognizable as clouds.
The sun must be setting for the colours offer'd.)
She is also wearing the aforemention'd uniform,
however hers is more form-fitting, while mine, slightly oversiz'd
makes me look broad shoulder'd and relaxed.
She has a small elfin face and huge eyes, fawn-like
in appearance, with a quick animation of the face
hovering silently between a defiant pout and
blonde blonde hair cut short against her skull
bright enough to see by but not blinding.
She had attitude and a beautiful ass.
I recognized immediately how obviously in love we
were obviously in love.

My father showed me the photo because I had given it to him as a
Christmas present a few years earlier when I had no money,
could afford little else, and thought perhaps he would enjoy learning
about his heritage. What better gift could there be?
It's sure funny how things come around.
And I was soon to meet my wife in person at her mother's house
after the war. It was New Year's Eve, I remember, and time
was prepared to stand still. God, in retrospect it was beautiful

when she came up the stairs from the sunken living room
(all the rooms were in shifting panels of brown and accents of soft orange;
the den contained curving plastic furniture against the wall
on the shag carpeting, and the local tv station was on, flickering
a news report about the little aliens). She looked about 14 and her
hair was still golden, even after all that time. She was such a tiny creature,
mayfly as in the photograph, and so happy to meet me, O! those eyes...
How hopelessly in love we were, finally comfortable in the peace of
one another's iron grip after being forced apart for so many years.

Let me tell you of how we were forced apart.

During dinner we couldn't stop casting glances across
the table and laughing nervously. The duck was absolutely
delicious, with an almost piscine appearance, and
tasting of chocolate mousse. Afterward, on our way to the
liquor store for provisions, from the back seat I heard
her say a sad joke about the size of her breasts, but I
didn't mind. I knew in time I would come to love her self-
destructive sense of humour. Picking her up at the
passenger door I carried her across the parking lot. Wind
blew all around us, shooting clouds back and forth, pushing the
sun into a tiny ball of post-war boom and drinking songs.
We didn't even know each other, regardless of whether the air
could actually disappear and dance menacingly across our
line of sight. We were just looking at each other, there;
and it was the happiest moment of our lives, all those eyes
no more than a foot away from one another and looking in.
Later we would come to realize (was it inside the liquor
store, between the French reds and the cann'd beer?)
that marriage is an art built on eye contact
that cannot stop because the hold never does.

Afterward we left the liquor store,
walking through the automatic door as it slid open,
bottles swinging and the presence of laughter, and on
the other side of the door we were divorced by reality.

◉ Perfectly Ordinary Dream #1620 (August 17, 1925)

The imagination could thrive in worse places of the world. It had become this particular newlywed couple's best interest to spend whole days hiding in the most expensive bookstores in town. No one ever bothered them there, and they were free to hug and kiss in the most exciting ways between the shelves. Occasionally they would browse through a poetry volume or two, but they found them dull and vile. They preferred returning to each other's company, perhaps foolishly over a blueberry muffin and apple juice at the snack counter. They were in love at each moment in the bookstore, happy to be holding hands and smiling, ignoring all the literature of the world. On one occasion, they both noticed Edward De Vere standing at one of the shelves, admiring one of his more recently published books. They exchanged a glance of concern. Both were wondering, as young couples might, why such a man would appear in this bookstore. Surely he was entirely out of place. In a room filled with characters dressed in the traditional neon colour'd garments of that country he seemed a parody of history wearing his sixteenth-century wool knickers and vest, the long ruffled Elizabethan coat and a pair of thin black leather shoes. Even his hairstyle added to his ridiculous costume. Somewhat longish, as though he were wearing a wig. It was tied at the back of his head with a velvet ribbon showing the weariness of age. The couple suddenly remembered the five dollars. They began to drift towards the door, shielding their faces as best they could with any available pamphlets, sticks, or newspapers. De Vere spotted them, however, and intercepted them in front of the store. He immediately demanded the return of his five dollars, exclaiming 'how is one to eat if everyone is constantly removing his money from his person!? A man has to eat, or poetry is nothing!' And he began slapping the young man about the face, though without any real violence, for when one is dealing with magic, violence can only be erotic. Despite this, the young man did in fact find himself growing somewhat annoyed, for De Vere squealed 'Five Dollars!' very loudly in a high-pitched voice for almost half an hour as he continued his assault. In a fit of exasperation, the young man suddenly tackled

Edward De Vere about the waist and lifted him (he was so light, the young man thought) upon his shoulders. And much to the rage and hollering of the great poet, ('five dollars! five dollars…!') the young man began to spin around and around on the sidewalk in front of the bookstore. The scene is very quiet. It is only the young man and Edward De Vere. No one else dares to enter the picture. At last the constant spinning became too much for the young man, and De Vere was ejected from his shoulders, landing in a crumpled heap in the gutter of the street where he lay for some time, until a smile surfaced on his ragged face. Standing, he straightened his collar (for he wore no tie) gave many thanks to the young man for his hospitality, and bid him good–day.

⊕ *Perfectly Ordinary Dream #254 (February 20, 1981)*

How sad the depression was. Yet, throughout it all, the 1930s were the light sparks of excitement rattling in his bones. All those decades riding the rails he never saw the poverty leave this world, and it was his conclusion that no one could survive it. He spent much of his time alone, speakeasy style, slipping from shadow to shadow along the night. His mind ready for anything, distracted by nothing, he was wearing the skirts of the past. The night so black it couldn't possibly exist. On the other side of the alley there is an invisible   wearing a brown down fill'd jacket and tie scrawling childlike words across a wall: 'Mr P. Cob_ / BEWARE'. The word BEWARE written in such a delicate calligraphy that it looks indecipherable, but our hero is ready to imagine it says anything, anything at all. How sad it is, he thinks, that throughout this dark hull of a city people are covering up each other's tracks. Painting over every artifact they can find in a quick attempt to claim it, to make it new and suitable to their own states of being. It all layers itself naturally, without any effort, and origin has no voice here. It is 1934 (it has been here for so long) and everyone is deep in the heart of a depression. Why does the rest of the world insist on becoming invisible at moments like these? Shaking his head at the invisible   who is still writing, he cannot believe the mind could shut down on itself, cannot believe there is anything worth saying about meeting exactly where our darkness covers up the tracks. In an instant he is ten feet back, and the invisible has sketched a square which is, he decides, the same size as the building on which it has been drawn. It is all very shocking. In an instant he is thirty feet back and the building is the same size as the sketch it is drawn on. And inside the square, he has noticed, is says nothing at all. In an instant he is seventy feet back and the man, still writing, is gone. And nothing happened.

✝ *Perfectly Ordinary Dream #1860[1] (July 9, 1969)*

We might as well be dead, and happy, and alive. It was the greatest reading he would ever give and as a blessing she was present. O the beauty of a single red head! This, too, would come to be an historic occasion, for it was the only time she would see William Blake read to an audience. At least she thought it was him up there on the stage. It was hard to tell, the way he hunched over himself, not even bothering to face the audience (of which she was the only member), his long wispy hair falling like curtains over his face, as though they might rise at any moment and the play would begin again. *A single table, centre stage, at which a man sits. A waitress appears (as though from nowhere) and takes the man's order. When she turns, the man watches her bum swaying away to the bar, and smiles to himself (for there is no one else in the bar). He pulls a revolver from his coat pocket. At the exact moment she begins to pull his beer, he shoots himself in the head.* The curtain falls. And William Blake remains hunch'd over his beer on the stage, reading his poems in the most clear, booming voice imaginable. It echoes around the empty room. There is not even a microphone. It is almost as though he does not wish his body to be present, only his voice. And she slowly begins to realize a most amazing sadness, she feels it bubbling up around the front of her skull: What sadness to have something to say, and no one who will listen. How sad and how beautiful the persistence, the sheer will to believe absolutely in what your mind can do. Another frothy beer appears on the table before her. No matter what brand she orders this same milky broth appears. Soap. Soap Milk. How strange, she thinks. Drunk out of her mind in the middle of the afternoon.

Perfectly Ordinary Dream # 1867 (January 21, 1932)

Rimbaud was not only surprised that the man standing before him wanted to publish his writing so adamantly, but that he didn't even recognize him as the author. 'This is the finest writing I have EVER laid my eyes upon', the man was saying (although he was of course speaking in French which is difficult to translate offhandedly). 'I have arrived as quickly as I could in order to publish it.' And he handed Rimbaud his favorite pieces of writing, one sheet at a time. Such were the many twists of fate he had experienced since he began working at the photocopy shop, and it was not the last. The author noticed that his publisher's tastes did not exactly coincide with his own, as he chose to publish work that was more flowery and wigged–out (as he had referred to it in his journal) than the outrageously violent pieces Rimbaud preferred. 'I wish to give copies of these to each one of my friends,' said the man. 'Please, if you are to help me.' Rimbaud placed the pages into the machine and printed fifteen thousand copies on recycled paper, each one stapled at the top left hand corner, as the man requested. He did not bother to say anything, but thought to himself how ridiculous it is to print fifteen thousand copies of anything, let alone some rambling scraps of writing done in fits of loneliness or exultation. But it was all in a day's work, he thought, and one must earn one's living at the expense of 'les feux de la monde'. He wasn't even pissed off that he had never given his consent to this man (was it a man? he wondered) to make free copies of his work to give to just anybody ('who knows who will read it?' said his excited publisher several times over the hum of the machine) but then again, Rimbaud hadn't bothered to get permission to write them either. At last the razor–sharp sound of the photocopier came to an end. In the dead silence that followed, Rimbaud handed the man his printing, took his money, and accepted one copy of his new book, for, as the man said, since they had done business together, they were now friends.

⊕ *Perfectly Ordinary Dream #1922 (December 12, 1954)*

As a young man, Cravan worked in the hippest libraries in town, both serving drinks and as a kind of mental co-ordinator. He was quite there in the sense that he had become accustomed to his own happiness, content to be earning a living doing something he rather enjoyed for a change. Hiding in the dark corners of rooms fill'd with books and journals, he could read telepathically what and as he pleased, his feet resting upon a shelf, a pen scrawling leisurely across one page or another. It all depended upon who he felt like BEING at any given moment, Miles Davis or Ezra Pound, Patrick Cobain or Drum Nick the sailor. Just then, the fat man sitting behind a large wooden desk began to complain loudly. Cravan was apparently not doing his job satisfactorily, and, well, admitted the clerk with a certain flabbiness, was simply not very good at doing anything at all. 'Fine!' shouted Cravan at the top of his bowel'd lungs, at first thinking he would simply quit the job altogether, then thought the better of it, for what else could there be to do with one's life? 'Here, sir, are your Maps!' He slammed the rolls of paper onto the sweating man's desk, scattering his charts and graphs, his pages and pages of accounted figures, everything flying into the air like so much dust. Throwing the lightest blow of his life to the man's face. Not even capable of denting the grin, Cravan turned on his heel and disappeared into the darkness forever.

Perfectly Ordinary Dream #1962 (September 17, 1985)

The fall couldn't even wake him up. Luckily,
the movie followed him down... in Slow
Motion. Easiest thing he ever done, ever.
Imagine waking up so deep in the gut, cover'd with
snow from the inside out but finding it warm. Then   [JOHN
imagine not waking up at all. There were so   BERRYMAN...]
many windows in the place when we moved there
it was no wonder that he fell, no wonder he couldn't
revive at that last possible second. And they say if you
die in a dream...
The dull angles of that
particular city were only dull, and grey, though
often bright and tempting at that time of the year.
We knew it as the slow motion of Hollywood and
football games what wore them out. I mean everyone,
not just the addicts. We could quite easily live in
this room forever now. There is such a nice view.
Only a little blood on the ankle, sticking out of the
broken windshield. And that's downstairs. It's so
fucking wonderful to follow the angels through an
open window, man, you float about three feet above them
all the way down. Facing the dopey expression
on these poets' faces can only be a parody of the great
literature of the world; it's just a little joke. Just
look at the great literature of the world. And at his hair
rustling in the wind, so vain in its attempt to be the air.
And the stillness of which is the world's greatest
poetry waiting patiently to be discovered.
Then imagine not waking up.

☉ Perfectly Ordinary Dream #1979 (May 4, 1996)

We could be as content as they. After several days of failed sexual intimacy they decided to throw a party. For fun they traded gender before the guests arrived, in order to explore one another's energy, and to learn a little more about themselves. Everyone was in attendance that evening, from the most famous of pop stars to the lowliest of poets, ghouls, and the like. They chose only to kill those of the literary genre. The first had been a harmless accident. The young woman had been dancing spasmodically to the sound of harps and razor-sharp violins, dubbed over by crickets, junebugs and something else (was it a solo praying mantis?) when she embraced William Blake so violently she snapped his neck. (For years to come the memory of the gentle pop that came to her ears in what seemed an eternity of silence followed by the folding of the man himself like a swan's last breath into her neck was enough to move her to orgasm.) After that it became more of an act of amusement to pick them off one by one during the course of the evening, then make up excuses as to their whereabouts. It was, after all, a rather boring party. ('Purdy? Why he's outside chopping wood again.' 'Christina Rosetti? Oh, she's in the can. Been in there a while too. I don't know what she's doing in there.' 'Tom Pynchon has been dead for years you fool!' and so on...) Of course the party had been days ago, and the bodies they had hung like silk garments on plastic coat hangers in the closet behind the bed were beginning to smell. The young man fretted. He had been in trouble with the local authorities before, and wanted not to repeat his mistakes. 'Fucking writers', he said one day, 'why do they have to stink so much? Can't they stay pure like glass at the bottom of the sea the way we've always been led to believe?' She would just giggle innocently and blow him a kiss. Every day he insisted they meet after work to discuss what to do. After all, what does one do with a bunch of literary corpses? But they were getting nowhere with these meetings, for each time their lovemaking became more and more intense. And the smell was getting worse. Finally, after a few weeks of mounting passion, they were surprised to discover that the young woman was pregnant (there was a certain look in her eyes), and they opened the closet to discover that nothing was left of the great writers. All that remained was this overpowering stench.

⊕ Perfectly Ordinary Dream #2000 (November 21, 1998)

Walter found that it was perfectly logical, actually, that she should appear on the other side of the counter today, so many years in the future, demanding his services in such a quiet voice she could barely be heard. Little Emily Dickinson. So far it had been an extremely dull week, so it was nice to see her again. He had not seen or heard of her since grade eleven. When they were children he had been quite smitten by her childish features. From what he remembered of his feelings towards her, they appeared to be born out of a grade 4 class photograph. (O, how many hours of longing grief had that picture caused! He smiled at the thought. She was seated only three heads away.) Why exactly he had been so attracted to her he had no idea, but it was there, and it had been something to believe in throughout his young days. Emily had never been able to show any interest in him at all, never able to comprehend his obsessions, Walter's sworn religion to her and her alone. Forever did Emily cast him from her sight with her vicious remarks, with the whips and the chains only she could cast from her beautiful poisonless mouth, the power she alone had to ignore him completely. And he would never forget the moment he suddenly knew that she had absolutely no interest in him at all. 'You just go on and on and on and on!' she had said. 'It's exasperatingly dull!' By high-school, Walter had given up believing in the power of his heart. Knowing that she would never be able to forget his youthful longings while in her presence, he discovered to his surprise that this gave him supernatural powers over her. Sitting across from her in chemistry class, he simply had to observe her reaction to the fact that they were together in the same room to know it was true. Using his voice to poke and prod, he found that he could shape her emotions into several unusual contortions they couldn't possibly have hoped to create without contact with an outside force. Especially a force that had already had a hand in their creation. It had been an interesting year for him, and he would not easily forget the lessons he had learned about the possibilities of love, of mind, and of grief. And today, years later, after no contact whatso-ever, Emily had returned, to ask something of him. Walter could not make out a single thing she was saying, only that there was a lovely music to her voice. It was the music he was presently conducting with his mind. WHAT IS IT EXACTLY THAT YOU WANT OF ME!! he knew he would yell at her as loud as he could over the noise of the radio, shouting directly into her eyes. Then he would refuse to serve her and send her away. But not just yet, he thought, asking her politely once again if she would mind repeating her request. For the sound of her voice was lovely, and he was enjoying themself, carefully playing her as though they were about to break.

☉ Perfectly Ordinary Dream #2198 (August 29, 1997)

'I know you were late for work this morning,' he exclaimed as John entered the photocopy shop. He took a huge bite of a hamburger. 'You must now fill out this form, so that I may attempt to have you fired.' His employer chomped again, though it didn't seem possible that he had finished the previous bite. John looked down at the fat and grease that was collecting on the front of his silk pink blouse. 'If you would like to appeal my decision', he said, biting at the same time, 'you may of course fill out the form on the reverse and submit it as well, but such an appeal can take up to a year to process.' He took another bite and John looked deep into the gaping hole. 'During this time you shall work here in this shop at no cost to me, your wages supplied by the taxpayers through the new welfare system.' *Ah, fuck it*, thought John, tearing up the silver piece of paper and placing it like a bib beneath the gaping hole as it continued to chew its most recent section of hamburger, *for the rest of the summer I thinke I'll take my chances and meditate peacefully upon the state of poverty that is most common in this part of the world.*
'I quit', he said. 'Suit yrself, loser', grunted his employer between bites. John Keats then left the photocopy shop. *Perhaps some daye he shall finde happiness. But I suppose by that time he will have reached the ende of his life, and the experience shall only be another waste of our most precious resource.* He wondered if he was really referring to all that paper he wasted on useless photocopies. 'A little of each', he said aloud as he opened the door and stepped outside into the sunshine as an unemployed bum for the first time in years, 'though I suspect that the waste of paper will have more of an effect upon the entire species.' He stretched as high as he could and breathed deeply. *Forget this gamey leg*, he thought, *I shalle walk all night if it is necessary*. And he started off down the street with a happy limp. 'It is nigh time I departed this place of back-stabbing pirates and greed.'
The sun was beginning to set. The streets were deserted except for the most valiant of hot dog vendors. Flashy, meaningless posters were plastered everywhere, each one advertising the most recent corporate scam. The maze had been maddening, but here it was only a sunset. What a ridiculous place in which to find our hero, the poet,

John Keats, surrounded by emblems of a world gone mad with forgetting. *Rotten Fuckers*, he decided, looking around, *poor frightened twisted fiends…* The souls of poets dead and gone… His limp grew worse. And he made his way home upon it. When he arrived hediscovered his old employer waiting for him in the back yard. He was down on his hands and knees and appeared to be praying, but he was only planting a small garden of paperclips for him, a whole nest of them, little silver creatures shining and squeaking. When he looked up John could tell he had been crying, saddened by something, but he wasn't sure if it was just the labour involved in planting the little shoots. 'It has been so difficult without you', the man bubbled softly from behind his soapy eyes, everything suddenly becoming lit by a glow that arose from the paperclips. 'Won't you please come back and write us a poem? I beg of you, please.' And he grasped his own hands before him in a prayer. 'No way', answered Keats, rising to the greatest height his gamey leg would permit. 'For thou hast maketh me to hayte the wordes that poureth from mye inky whole. I giveth up all words from this daye forward to become insteade a saylor of the waters of the whorle.' And he left the pleasant garden scene and mayde his waye, lymping downe to the sea.

Perfectly Ordinary Dream #2748 (August 6, 1988)

Regarding the calligraphy of this parchment
she knew she was looking at the work of a true artist.
It's always nice to receive a letter from the heaven, isn't it?
The flowing lines were so precise, and the ink blots
connecting each moment had been placed an interval
that gave the overall piece a perfect balance.
Nothing of it could possibly be interpreted in any way
('Dear Death, hello'). The occasional 'h' found along
the margin of the work seemed to have a specific
reference to the past, to a lost culture, one splattered
against the new language that had been emerging
from the hills, and during a particularly interesting reading
she realized that each of these symbols appeared in lower case.
While thinking the capital suggested a crossing
over (having the physical appearance of a bridge), along
a beam stretching between two states of being, now joined,
(these poles who remain apart are separated only by death)
the lower case could only suggest an attempt that failed
miserably in any way to communicate

beginning from the left and falling short
of any connection with the right
left to decipher all the
beautiful unreadable calligraphy

Perfectly Ordinary Dream # 3097 (June 30, 1973)

They all found it wonderful, living in an attic by the seaside, rearranging the furniture. His wife was there, as was God, (of course) and several friends who would sometimes pose nude near the window while he painted, their forms becoming more and more like shapes in the yellow of the sun. Van Gogh himself had recently taken to wearing leather biker jackets and smoking American filterless cigarettes. It was 1977, the summer almost over, lazy, lost, turning golden and slightly mad with hope. Everyone content to live by the sea breathing deep lungfulls of saltwater air from dawn till dusk. And on weekends they could go to the fair! God had designed the attic, since Her room was just off to one side, and She acted as an omnipotent landlord of sorts. In the evenings, after sunset, the entire group would gather here to watch Van's latest television like a painting. (He insisted we all call him Van, as though he wanted to become a parody of his younger self, grown hip in the August of life.) It was the only way they knew how to do it. No one was aware of it, but he was painting secret rooms for them, places where everyone could live and where nothing made sense. How often had we all dreamed of those rooms! Everyone was finally becoming comfortable, able to ease into their own skin. The breezy days of summer had come to realize that a red stroke was perhaps a fine toenail. Or a brown one an eyeball, looking at your tits or cock as you lazed in the golden window. Or this blue smudge was the sky covered with flecks of small green birds over the ocean. But the yellow was always the sun. Of this we were certain. Deep down we all wondered how long would it take us to figure out he was so full of shit? Only his wife knew what he was really up to, and she wasn't saying anything, preferring to sit quietly beside him holding his frail, bone-like hands. She didn't mind his recent affairs at all, but she would often turn to look for the secret doorway in the corner.

☉ Perfectly Ordinary Dream #3522 (February 14, 2014)

It was very nice for us to have met Nietzsche's father at the olde house where the philosopher had grown up. And to discover that he was now younger than his own sonne despite the diagnosis that had left him riddled with a terminal cancer! These days he was aging backward through time. This was obviously the only logical solution, and we could tell he was happy to oblige. Our friend still seemed in awe of his father's full head of long curly hair after all those years of baldness. It fell past his shoulders now, and the white whiteness of his grin, a kind of smile really, no, actually it was a smile come to think of it, a real smile, one that had seen beyond the picturesque view of his own existence now that his sonne had finally come to visit. At any rate, it was nothing at all like his sonne's grimace. The two of them were rapidly moving in different directions now, away from each other through the moments of their dissent. And this was fine to us, people outside their circle of birth and regeneration, a group of onlookers who happened upon the two of them when the psychology of our age could no longer apply on an individual level. And they were so cute sitting in their chairs, his father's indicated by a sign which read 'Nietzsche's Chair' and the following inscription:

> *We sat together for hours, sipping lemon lager on the rooftop. Each of us offered an idea in regard to approaching the world in absolutely human terms, one side pushing the against the boundaries of happiness and despair, the other shrinking into the absolute of perseverance. 'Keep it simple', said his father, 'It is the nature of the world to protect all fools'. Each of them went through the family photo album in the sunshine, one page at a time, telling each story in the shade of the trees.*

☧ *Perfectly Ordinary Dream #4127 (March 30, 1928)*

The rollerskating was fine, and Ray had the knack, but somehow
it just felt like running, nothing special. What he expected to happen
and what was actually happening were two polarized events that
could occur simultaneously, much like the past and the future,
being only shadows of the present, could occur
in a shared moment where neither exists. It was a calculated addiction.
Tomorrow, in the bar, she became suicidal, turning up the air con-
ditioner as high as it would go. Several of the customers became
white with grief beneath the permafrost, looking like drunken ghosts
of people he once knew. She insisted that he drink glass after glass of
fine scotch, even though she knew he would only make himself sick.
'I am in the middle of a CRISIS', she exclaimed, and ordered him
another drink. Ray wanted to know what was the matter, and in
response she ordered him another drink. 'When it comes to poetry',
she finally said, 'there is no such thing as time. It is all of time meeting
in a bar at the same time.' He decided it was stupid to be there.
Meanwhile, in another room of the mansion, Sal was discussing his
upcoming wedding with his fiance Lyllith, his mother-in-law, and Ray.
'The Female Spirit shall surely outlive the male spirit', said Sal. 'And
considering how it is that I live, considering how stupid is my life, I don't
suppose I can afford this marriage presently. Perhaps at a future time.'
And he vanished as quickly as Ray had appeared in the room. Outside Ray
wondered what he had done to deserve this, for it seemed his friend would
only propose marriage to young beautiful women in order to tell them
about the female spirit. Was he trying to instruct them? he wondered.
Was he trying to lure them away from the vacancy of fashion? Ray and
his wife laughed long and hard over that one, and he took her hand in his.
'We should call you Man too', he said earnestly. They walked through the
snow to their car, each flake falling into that dream in which he had lost the key.

Perfectly Ordinary Dream # 4301 (December 31, 1999)

Kurt's party was a great success. Everyone he knew was present, his wife Gwendolyn, wearing her wedding dress, her family and friends arriving via motortrain around the bonfire (thoughtfully prepared by the best man). His family and friends were already present, seated upon the available cushions, drinking beer, listening to the percussionist slapping rhythms upon his thigh. One guy we met thought he had an in because we were in the wedding party, but when we introduced him he only embarrassed us, telling Kurt he could take him places, make him a huge star. He went on and on about a brilliant man at the beginning of his career. We actually had to steer him away from the guest of honour, explaining to him that our deaths are far more important events in our lives than anything leading up to them; how we choose to face that frontier is our only reason for living. 'Now leave Him be', we said in unison, 'for he is busy living'. It was a great speech, and everyone fell silent while Kurt hammed it up with baby Francis. Around midnight we heard the clocks banging, and someone threw a half-filled beer bottle through the window. As it splattered on the asphalt below, a drunken gunman, who had been waiting all night for a chance to demonstrate his songwriting abilities, appeared at the window and began firing at Kurt Oswald. Bullet holes appeared about his head as would a halo, holding the wild, triumphant look in his eye. A signature photograph, if ever there was one. Neither Gwendolyn, nor baby Francis let out a scream, but looked on with admiration. This, after all, was their family reunion. Kurt finally slumped in his chair, gambler style, and we all said goodnight, to Kurt as well, who thanked us for coming, (he shook our hands most vigorously, although I admit there was something odd about it), until the gun-man accidentally shot out the light and we watched death throes seen only by strobelight.

☉ *Perfectly Ordinary Dream #4555 (July 7, 1997)*

In one of Pound's lost polaroids we find a cat in the shape of a human dancing. It is a black cat against a black background, absolutely grotesque, a puppet of souls. In another, there is an infant sleeping, accompanied by a simple melody: 'kyrie, kyrie, kyrie…' In a third among the hundreds lost, there is a potted flower sitting beneath the photocopied page from bissett's *Sailor*, pinned to the watercolour of a spaceship beside the shelf holding the radio and a collection of compact discs and tapes. You can listen to the music. On the other side of the window hangs a bird feeder where sparrows and other small birds, as yet unnamed, gather to take the seed. Each one of them holds a polaroid in their beak, an entire flock of clouds. Pound's polaroids were lost at sea, and at the present time, not one of them has been found.

Perfectly Ordinary Dream: An Essay (January 13, 1971)

Everyone needs a Book Thug. In fact, every publishing company should adopt a Book Thug, and then we'd see what could become of the industry in this country:

> It was so exciting now that his new imaginary publishing company, Book Thug, had produced a first edition of poems. He had been out of his mind for weeks, planning it into being, and now that the imaginary deluxe edition by some obscure poet who had already received her half of the profit had hit the streets, manuscripts were pouring in from every obscure writer he could imagine.

While other publishing companies busy themselves producing massive quantities of identical textual material, in often boring and unattractive physical states, Book Thug only produces imaginary books in small editions, say between fifty to one hundred copies. (Oo! there's one now!) Each one is an original, hand-made copy, and a delight to behold. Not only that, Book Thug splits the edition (the profit) with the author instead of paying her the usual ten percent royalty:

> He did not feel cheated in any way that the author of the book had received exactly half of the print run as payment. He had merely built an acceptable piece of architecture for the author's conception of a language, so both of them had had an equal responsibility to the finished product.

The question as to the success of an imaginary publishing company such as Book Thug lies only in the number of people who are willing to adopt it. Call it what you will, and when you do, and act upon it, you will discover both the freedom it offers, and the problems it presents, at any of the National Book Fairs, for instance, or in journals of literary review. The best thing to do in this case is to remain as imaginary as possible and let culture continue to battle at will:

> The author was overjoyed with her half of the Book Thug edition. In fact, she was so pleased, that she herself had began producing her own imaginary publications under the name Ten O'Clock Sharp. In just under a week she had built just under seven beautiful editions, and had distributed them accordingly: fifty percent here, fifty percent there, always placing her half of the profit on a shelf she had built specifically for that purpose. But it was becoming tiresome to have to explain to anyone who happened to visit her bookshop that the shelf was not empty. Exactly why people couldn't see her books she could not imagine.

♁ Hazel's Dream (you are now in the present, reading)

In Hazel's Dream she is not only a part of the world, but she is the world, a whole planetary moment of breath and anguish and love, here for her own sake as the planet is. When I saw the words 'Legalize Freedom' scrawled across the bathroom wall of a restaurant some weeks ago, I thought immediately of her, wanting to be permitted her own stride during her time here without fear from the tyranny of assholes et cetera. Or if she couldn't be the Planet, perhaps she could become a part of it without the sudden afterthought that others around her will think her wrong or stupid or unsympathetic. In other words, the freedom to participate wherever she may be upon whatever mind she feels free to be, without making enemies in the process. Even if she chooses to be uncomfortable with her surroundings. For me, language is an entire planet, every angle of existence seems hinged upon it. I have become a part of a planet where freedom of speech is the natural product of experience. My general state of grief comes from spending my working days in a place where such a phenomenon is not only unappreciated, but does not exist. As D said when he stopped by one morning to drop off the posters for the Scream, I'm deep behind enemy lines, but because of the language (the planet, in all its ongoing possibilities) life there is bearable, and at the same time I can observe Success from a safe distance where I can learn the details without the pressures of being involved. In Hazel's Dream we are all involved, everyone is on their own private level, interacting safely and with vigorous appeal for the future of human knowledge, happiness and the like. No matter what we do we are all allowed to do it, no matter what we choose we have chosen it. There are no real sides other than the ones we carry in our minds. In Hazel's Dream we start to work on those dividing lines, borders that never existed in the first place until those pesky humans came along. I have met at least nine incarnations of my wife to date, and I have to admit that each one of them has been incredibly patient while the drunken orangutan was writing, but you should see all of them walk into a room together, no one on this planet could hope to write like that.

Notes

1 Note to POD # 1860: lives cannot be of any other being, only our own, until it becomes confused by the ongoing commentary of sexuality. (kiss me, kiss me you angel you beast) but because of our sudden admiration, where it may appear, we are often amazed that anything exists at all beyond the sensations we experience as they occur. And with all these beauteous forms, who must be considered at all costs, we shall bite the nails of lifeand die. Blake's craggy deep opens upward. there is no place else for it to go.

James Llar was born in Edmonton, Alberta, in 1971, and moved to Toronto when he was 30. He lives near High Park with his wife Emma, a librarian and bookseller. Two previous books, *The Sun Is So Dark* (1998), and *Wharts* (2001), have appeared from Coach House Books.

portrait of James Llar by Alex Cameron

short ghosts

John Elliott

COACH HOUSE BOOKS　　　TORONTO

Remember childhood smallness

forever witchcraft,
openness, and a life

(alive) (eyes)
was they both looking out?

when could i tell the difference
between the small & now

specific points are so small
to the deity of tome

speak such a small language
says we are anything at all

    J.M.

❦ Suicide Note on My Wedding Day

come & sit a while
I want to talk to you forever

things will always
never be the same

🌹 Heaven[1]

everyone is so asleep all the time
aren't we such agile sleepwalkers

🌹 Hell[2]

everyone is so asleep all the time
aren't we such agile sleepwalkers

❦ Bike Poem 3

on the bike

moving's pace

🌸 Van Gogh's Irises

are so blue against

taking a piss

the burgundy wall

into the toilet

there to receive

into the visions of it

Long Playing Record

the child's first memory
would of course be the rain
falling out of the sun
& into the sky & at
the exact moment it touches
the earth evaporating

❦ Untitled*

This poem is called FUCK YOU & is dedicated
to all those whose tyranny & greed will forever
spill me into contemplations of living poverty
within the trenches of stress, which is
Satan's realm for these, the tears of our
present torment, as our hopes & joys,
happiness & the like, are struck down
in these the years of our lives, the core of which is now,
& tomorrow, & for all time. Someone is yelling
at me about the present. It is not my fault. As long as the
flood of the violent awash the land & work their ways
against the useless & stupid golden sun
utopian dreams of our ancestors. These, all blazen
with colours/feelings/conversations & the like
C O M M U N I T Y
the manifold of beauty in our otherwise meaningless lives,
WE ARE ALL GOD FOR THEIR SAKE
\/\/\/\/\
they all become stressed to the point of non-being
here inside the lurching shine of false democracy
fake/fake/fake

(tyranny/democracy/greed)

Vote Now

❦ Of Joy & in Sadness

There's a particular brand of rain
Music that falls through the old radio

Joy of falling without worry
Landing exactly where you meant to
Listening to Rachmaninoff & the rain

🌹 Down Near The Creek Where The Rainbow Trout

walking beside the creek dad
points out how the setting is made
entirely of its components
just by being there it seems &
I declared the experience of nausea
in what appeared to be a spoken language
& everything
immediately witnessed was necessary
to disappear within myself
until the experience
&
I puked till I felt better
sorta digested spaghetti coating
the autumn goldenrod
quite a surprise no an honest shock
to find it there
the glistening sway
within the scenery
&
each of the components
one after the other
turn around as I turn around
that sweep
took them all in again
climbing up from the edge of the creek
over & over
until I am gone

dad waits there chewing tobacco

What It's Like

balanced precariously the half shells of broken eggs
each containing the yolk of a slightly larger species
the delicate squashed membrane bleeds perfectly within itself
walking upon them is much like falling over
without fear in your heart
of the possibility within each one of becoming a whole collection

i was concerned with my political state upon waking
that my first thought was of this language & in it itself everyday

🌹 Eclipse

I have not perhaps
remembered

seeing your eyes
for days

aloneliness
messinessness

two fried eggs:
eatin em right out of the pan

eatin right outofa sway the middle
of the kitchen floor has now

taste?
no, i don't think so

stupid plastic yellow & white
hunger so dull you just fill it

another day coming to end
darken into light decay

where you are what you
are doing tonight

On Imitation

after Jay MillAr

I remember having to give
a talk for a philosophy class on
'the sonnet' & not having
time to reseach anything
wrote all the poems himself
& placed the names
of famous writers
at the bottom of each page
except the one by Shakespeare
for he is the source of all imitation
a cliché sadly
& what we must all become

spend a good hour talking
about them in the third person

❦ *Looped*

:

the

city

to

repeat

or

restrict

the

:

Liz Phair

the birds have started using the feeder at last
small bodies the size of each feather made to
shift variously as angels other than themselves

regarded one eye at a time, stealing seeds & glances
through the dirty window language pulls at the air
of gravity along a line of the planet flying
then silence caught up in the frenzy of sunlight

New B r e a th

what wanted to say something
to yr voice (the theme of any telephone
connection always so fucking over
whelming) your voice after all & strong,
enough of everything to reach
yr form, being an aura, wherever
it is & what it is doing (a magnetic
pull, toward the sound itself) the
silence of noise as it is resounded:
H E L L O...
& I can think of anything at all
'pon that breath (for what are tears,
really, but what they truly are) a
vacant emotion & noise to come
out of, (refraction in the
purest sense) the very most human
in & of

🍺 *BeerTour*

Tuesday morning glory in absolute sunshine & I remember
being near traintracks positive no clouds were there

Somewhere between St Mary's & London
the radio too describes early nineties pop musicalism
to the rumble of the engine the five of us are on
& the back seat is stacked with bottles of beer

Spring almost present in the blue blue sky
& the air so light & lengthening I will remember always
the shine of melting snowbanks close to blinding & the smell of them
where we stopped to take a piss

Dirt road's gravel & the spring melt there
pebbles gathered under us as the scenery chants
a memory or postcard & memory as it happens in ways
flimsy but incredibly perfect & placed openly above

Drunk in the fine weather or at least totally sober
finally in the lengthening days of spring
& feeling that for once we were who we are
yes alive   blue, white, & moving calm
calm as the sun
& clean as the blue blue sky

Even the cops there are friendly
& give everyone tickets they will never have to pay

🌹 Home

(taken from a notebook)

The Home, an extension of your skin. The Home, it draws breath, exhales, pumps its own blood. The Home has shape, it consumes daily, excretes daily. The home radiates internally, like the human heart, an angel. It sings space familiar.

The things of your offering make up its shape, its hospitality. You own its design through the very thought you had to place this photograph here, a bookshelf there. You make a space feel safe, comfortable, like a warm shower. It is the place where you return, where you eat, where lovers meet in the night. It is where human secrets can live easily, where human stories are born. Mythology.

Moving from a space lived in over a long period of time into another space is traumatic, like removing one's body & replacing it with another. I'm sure it's not all that different than a terrible scar received in an automobile accident that heals, replenishing the skin, mending itself into a similar shape, not entirely the same as it was before. But the things remain the same, are joined by new things. There is a shift in consciousness delicate enough to allow for human growth. One changes slightly to accommodate the new space, as does the space to accommodate you.

It is harder to sleep in a new space for the first few weeks. This is the transitional period. You cannot sleep how you used to sleep, dream the dreams you used to have. The sheets are different, they have a new texture, the sounds are more quiet, the direction of the wind coming in through the window is from another part of the world. The window itself is bigger or smaller, the position of the moon & the stars are not the same. This transitional period is actually a dream in which you find yourself in a new territory, an altogether different part of the universe.

Imagine what creatures dwell there. What myths you will write. How it will grow.

🌹 Bazooka

Life is not tedious. Life is not boring.
Each day is not a mindless repeat of the last.
The people in your life are not stupid/uncaring/thoughtless.
Your apartment is not a mess. The laundry is not
A chore. The dishes are not boring. Your cat will
Not die. Life is not tedious. You are not depressed.
Today is not the same as yesterday/last week/a year ago.
Life does not tire you out. You are not stressed out.
The city is not dirty. People do not die. You are
Not angry. You are not lonely. Days do
Not repeat. Humanity is not pointless. Death
Is not real. The city is not ugly. Life is not a
Mindless repeat of the last. Boredom does not exist.
No one shall ever come to any harm.

🌸 Humanism (part vii)

(parts i-vi are yours)

we can open up all those vents
only to find out how easily they close
in on us in the end. we like it that way

its so very irresponsible not to pay attention
to those fingers basking in the sunlight

every night i go home & run along your skin
it makes me happy to be human with you
owning fingers, & lips too, toes & pubic hair

just imagine what
those other hidden parts

🌺 Our Honey Moon

what the hell
this postcard has no edges

but this music definitely has longing
& being inside the water has our songs

as passionate as hate i love your songs
now come to bed & sing of longing

come here now have no edges
in heaven's postcard some other space is hell

can break through & be Love as well

❦ Firelight

makes
all conversation
song or story

tell me the centre
around everything
in the mind-like dark

look in
get lost

❦

crawl upward

a long spine
to the tip
of the skull

scared of
the stars that way
no light can

look out
get lost

Workin' Stiff

ride out the day
get paid

ride outa here
get beer

❦ Jan 31 Mythologized on Feb 2

We all sat at the table drinking beer
drawing the cover to an imaginary apolitical magazine
& were joined from time to time by other spirits with similar names
who would disappear quietly scraping their empty chairs

when the lights went down John got up to use the phone
& Stef started apologizing to me all over again so i knew he was drunk
our minds have been hinged upon that moment of the apology for months
& it's so fucking tiring
i often fall asleep at that moment & dream the rest of the encounter for days

i always seem to notice afterwards that moment
when the slight tilt to his appearance comes

the aggressive remarks flying out of the tabletop to the drumbeat of his voice
would not help during the coming mornings
to smooth over a year long rent in the collective position we had invented
in the years leading up to my wedding
& has continued since then to build aggressive positions
between myself & my wife
but that's been saved for the latter portion of the evening

he accuses me of various emulations on my part which i felt was ridiculous
as i was perfectly aware of them
& he began to float away then
in the form of several well known minimalist discourses
& i became suddenly very heavy
& i drifted away from the situation & out into the street

walking through the dark snowing evening a voice came to me out of the traffic
the usual hallucination all over again that never realized before
just how solid he had ever been
butting his head with mine across a table cover with spilled beer & ashes
now he lives only in my memory like everyone i ever knew
& i hear his voice calling to me today with the casual
      disintegration of the past

❦ Within Finity

sitting with her
always like sitting
with infinity

as it has been for some time now,
& it spins in a gold liquid,
around, alive & dead.

Ghosts are the ghosts
of language & mindful of such
this scarlet nihilism

might crease the very thought,
O crevice   deep
in the shadows where we are

we give up the ghost into the air
of ourselves, of the actual,
on breath gathered

in a random order
gathered to be released
& in which all possible
moments are full of hope

take this gold liquid
o crevice, which is both
Alive & Dead, &

smooth our hands
in the infinite breath of our relative
crinkle of shimmering air

sitting without a coffin
within finity gathered
inside the liquid & golden
scarlet voice

🏵 Canadian Visionary

Poetry Americana for the cynics,
critics, those who have lived life sadly &
in part. Read Brits. Wake, up.
Read the works of visionaries

& hope. Canadian literature
sleeping. Sleeps. And dreams.
The dream / Read
American poetry & suffer

WHAT?
Read. O read. O poem.

What in the World is Coming to

& we were dreaming of becoming in a world
wracked by misery & desolation, hurt & death.

& we were dreaming of becoming pure energy.

& we were dreaming of becoming love when there
was no love, of becoming hate to fill the void.

& we were dreaming of becoming light.

& we were dreaming of becoming a dream,
dark erotic visitations to each other.

& we were dreaming of becoming root.

& we were dreaming of becoming magic
incantations of a planet bathing us in warmth.

& we were dreaming of becoming warm.

& we were dreaming of becoming
something in the deep beautiful blue.

& we were dreaming of becoming

Endnotes

1 We only use 10% of our total brain mass for a reason.

2 We only use 10% of our total brain mass for a reason.

3 'If it were not for this poem I doubt that I would ever ride a bicycle in the city of Toronto. It is the only thing I can remember to swerve in & out between the violent auto drivers. Whenever I drive a car I notice the televisionesqueness that haunts the mind, & I am sure that many people who drive regularly never quite know where they are, which would explain the high number of deaths occuring in our city as the transit drivers crush yet another sweet Taoist rider. Why must violence be everywhere? Please remove the cars from the city core & let us all breathe. Imagine! Yonge Street a six-lane highway right to the lake.'

    J.M.

John Elliott lives in Toronto, Ontario, where he is Writer In Residence at Print T[h]ree (University & Wellington franchise). His wife Hazel is a choreographer, dancer and novelist. Together they have created many collaborations, including Saffron, Claire, & Aiden.

portrait of John Elliott by Alex Cameron

Typeset, printed and bound at the Coach House on bpNichol Lane, Toronto, Ontario, M5S 2G5
The first edition of twenty boxed copies and four hundred trade copies was printed in
May of 2000.

The paper is Zephyr Antique Laid.
All artwork by Alex Cameron
Boxes for limited edition hand-made by Don Taylor
Editor for the Press: Victor Coleman
Copy edited and designed by Darren Wershler-Henry

To read the online version of *The Ghosts of Jay MillAr*, visit our website at:
www.chbooks.com

To add your name to our e-mailing list, write:
mail@chbooks.com

Typeset in Cartier Book. In January 1967 the graphic designer Carl Dair released Cartier, the first text typeface to be designed in Canada. In 1999, Rod McDonald reworked the roman, finished the italic and added a bold weight. He incorporated many changes necessary to produce a working text face for digital typesetting.